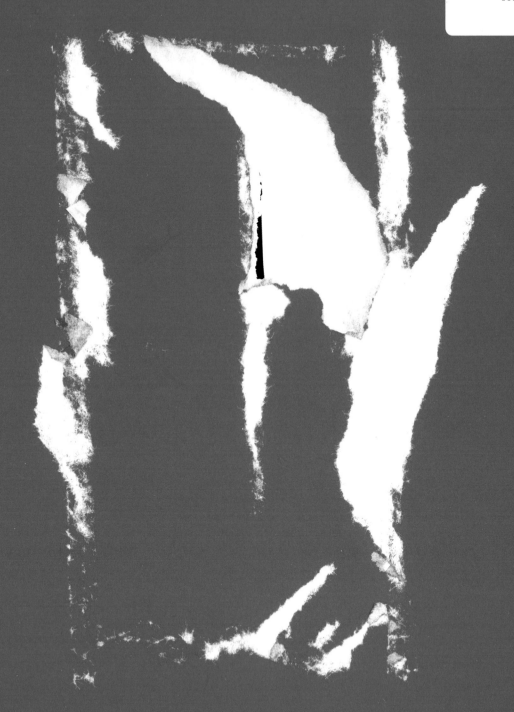

Wines of
ITALY

ISBN 88-89272-07-4

This book was conceived, edited and designed by McRae Books Srl
Borgo Santa Croce, 8 - 50122 Florence, Italy
info@mcraebooks.com

Project Director: Anne McRae
Design Director: Marco Nardi
Text: Kate Singleton
Photography: Diego Banchetti (all, except bottles)
                 Studio Lanza, Walter Mericchi (bottles)
Layouts: Yotto Furuya
Editing: Anne McRae
Colour separations: Fotolito Toscana, Florence

Printed in Italy by Artegrafica, Verona

Kate Singleton

Wines of SICILY

Photography by Diego Banchetti

with a Foreword by Diego Planeta

McRAE BOOKS

Table of Contents

Foreword

I was happy and somewhat flattered to be asked to write this introduction, even though at the time I still hadn't actually looked through what I knew would prove to be a very fine book.

I accepted the invitation partly because I knew Kate Singleton and her work, and was sure I wouldn't be disappointed. However, I was also spurred on by my own relentless enthusiasm for Sicilian winemaking.

The publication itself is not overly weighty, yet it provides the reader with a colourful and effective overview of the major oenological revolution that Sicilian producers have managed to achieve in recent years.

"From Quantity to Quality" truly sums up current Sicilian viticulture. To paint such an accurate and indeed enticing picture of the island's wines and the men and women who make them must have required a great deal of protracted field work. The many factors that underlie a good bottle of wine are here brought to the fore with great insight and considerable communicative skill.

I try to imagine myself as a non-Sicilian coming across this book, and I realise that it would draw me to the island like a magnet. Not only would I want to taste the wines, but also see with my own eyes the landscapes from which they derive, and perhaps meet the people whose faces and voices are captured in these pages.

Suffice it to mention a few of the images to be savoured ahead: the "simple, microscopic lichens that take on the goliath of petrified lava, gradually preparing a bed for the wild fennel and broom that will take root and, over the centuries, help break down the rivers of dark rock until they become friable, mineral-rich soil"; or the "Wild flowers that grow in astounding profusion, their colours uniquely intense. Common species are as though magnified beyond all recognition, so that daisies almost appear to be dahlias."

Add to such pictures wines whose "general hallmark is elegance, plus a gratifying element of divertimento" and the reader is ready to set sail.

So let me steal no more time from the reader, and instead address the author: Kate, you have fallen in love with Sicily, so come back as soon as you can. I know you still have plenty more to write.

DIEGO PLANETA

7

Introduction

From Quantity to Quality

Wine drinkers around the world have been enjoying Sicilian wines for decades. Most of them, however, have been unaware of it. Until recently, the island's massive output consisted largely of strong bulk wines (sometimes even grape concentrates) that were shipped off to central and northern Italy and France in vats to imbue local products with the muscle they lacked. Though most producers would probably deny it, many a Tuscan, Piedmontese and Burgundy wine has benefited from this injection of southern temperament.

Yet in recent years this somewhat servile and anonymous oenological image has undergone radical change. Across the island Sicilian winemakers have come to realise not only that their future lies in quality, but also that in this pursuit they are uniquely blessed with an abundance of the right ingredients: a warm, dry climate, a variety of suitable soils, a wealth of interesting indigenous grape varieties and a vocation for winemaking that dates back to the arrival of the Ancient Greeks in Sicily during the mid 8th century BC.

The outcome is a growing number of wineries, some of them small but many of them large by Italian standards, that have shifted their focus to concentrate on producing wines of remarkable finesse and character at relatively reasonable prices. These include a few of the *cantine sociali*, or large cooperative wineries, that held sway in the days of bulk wines. For them it was a question of opting for quality or gradually going out of business. By providing their growers with the necessary expertise in the vineyard and investing in appropriate technology and a proven oenologist in the cellar, they have been able to ride on the crest of change. Indeed, huge wineries like Settesoli at Menfi and the lesser but still large Cantine Sociali di Trapani have greatly contributed to the strength of the wave.

Whatever their size, the hallmark of these wineries is individuality. This even comes to the fore using the international grape varieties. A well made Sicilian Cabernet Sauvignon or Chardonnay tends to transcend predictable international models simply because microclimate and soil will, happily, never conform.

In Sicily these factors vary enormously, since grapes are grown from the coast with its torrid climate and sandy soils to the cooler climes and volcanic, mineral-rich soils of Mount Etna. With its nearly 26 thousand square kilometres, Sicily is the largest and most populous island in the Mediterranean, accounting for 17.5% of Italy's vineyards. And while the image of snow-capped Etna, enflamed by molten lava, has reached television audiences across the globe thanks to the visual impact of recent eruptions, it requires a certain conceptual effort to appreciate that Pachino, the municipality in the province of Siracusa in the south-eastern tip of the island that is currently attracting major investment in viticulture, actually lies further south and is thus hotter and more arid than north African cities such as Tunis.

Alessio Planeta, who heads the trail-blazing winery of the same name, rightly declares that "Sicily is a continent when it comes to wine". He then goes on to point out that his two major wineries, one at Menfi near Agrigento and the other one further south east

⋂ The laboratory at the Cantine Settesoli cooperative winery at Menfi facilitates the logistics of harvesting through to fermentation and ageing, thus ensuring quality control of a vast output.

⊃ ⊃ Contrasting landscapes: winegrowing in the arid soils of Licata in the south west; and the verdant rolling hillsides of the Tasca d'Almerita estate at Regaleali, inland between Palermo and Caltanissetta.

down the coast and slightly inland at Noto in the province of Ragusa, belong to different viticultural universes. "Though hardly distant if you look at the map, the difference between them is like the difference between Piedmont and Tuscany".

So Sicily is like several regions rolled into one. Add to such natural resources grape varieties like the red Nero d'Avola or the white Grillo, to mention but two of the many indigenous to Sicily and practically unheard of elsewhere, and you have a range of tastes, aromas, colours and hues probably unequalled by any other single production region in the world.

No wonder Sicily is currently being hailed as Europe's most promising quality wine-producing region. As such it has been attracting some substantial investment on the part of winemakers from other regions of Italy: wine magnate Gianni Zonin from the Veneto now owns Feudo Principi di Butera, of which he is rightly proud; another Venetian industrialist, Paolo Marzotto, is creating a magnificent winery at Baglio di Pianetto near Palermo; and the

Mezzacorona Group from Alto Adige, up near the Austrian border, has cut no corners in rebuilding and replanting the Feudo Arancio estate at Sambuca di Sicilia, near Agrigento.

At the 2004 edition of Vinitaly, the major wine fair held annually in Verona, hordes of visitors, many of them wine professionals, flocked to the Sicilian Pavilion. Unlike the Tuscan Pavilion, there were no stands designed to look like castles, no rhetoric or show. Instead, an atmosphere of patient, self-confident measure prevailed. It was as though the Sicilians were showcasing their island's potential rather than competing with each other.

Over the past ten years, participation by Sicilian wineries at the international wine fairs (Düsseldorf, Bordeaux and Turin as well as Verona) has quintupled. Acclaimed producers such as Tasca d'Almerita, Rapitalà and Donnafugata, whose wines have long had a following well beyond the confines of Sicily, are now joined by younger and often smaller companies who have achieved widespread recognition. Planeta is the most evident case in point,

◐ *Alessio Planeta.*

↻ *Zibibbo vines growing close to the ground in hollows dug into the volcanic soil of the island of Pantelleria.*

rating 19th with its *Chardonnay 2000* in Wine Spectator's 100 best wines for 2002. Fazio Wines, Abbazia Santa Anastasia, Morgante and Cusumano, to name but a handful, also have far-flung admirers; and not far behind are myriad other inventive upholders of quality and individuality who are destined to make their mark in coming years.

Less than twenty years ago, Sicily's 202,000 hectares of vineyard produced an annual 10 million hectolitres of wine. By 1995 the vineyards had dropped to just over 144,000 hectares, whereas the output had increased to 10.391,000 hectolitres. With an eye on the bulk market, growers were planting high-yielding grape varieties that produced anonymous wines whose only virtue was their strength. Six years later, output had dropped to just over 7 million hectolitres, with only a small decrease in the vineyard area. The search for quality at the expense of quantity was under way.

So what brought about such an impressive change of heart? Much of it is attributable to the far-sighted policy enacted by the Sicilian Regional Institute for Viticulture and Wine (*Istituto Regionale della Vite e del Vino*). Fully aware that wine-drinkers the world over were drinking less, but better and with greater discernment, this institution became a centre for information, advice and research. Not only did it provide growers with the appropriate expertise regarding planting and pruning for quality, but it also focused winemakers' attention on the importance of modern vinification techniques, including the use of cooling technology, barriques, bottle ageing and so on.

In its heyday, the *Istituto Regionale della Vite e del Vino* also went several steps further, planting a number of experimental vineyards throughout the island to test the potential of French grape varieties, of varietals from mainland Italy and of Sicily's own rich heritage of native stock.

Though these "*campi sperimentali*" have been radically reduced in number in the last few years, they have served the purpose of alerting growers to possible new horizons in wine production.

♪ *Highly automated bottling plants are now the rule even in smaller wineries.*

⮑ *Ripe Nero d'Avola grapes just prior to harvesting.*

Montenero

🏠 Abbazia Santa Anastasia

🍾 IGT – red wine aged for 12 months in barriques and 12 months in the bottle

🍇 Nero d'Avola 60% Merlot 20%, Cabernet Franc 20%

🕐 5–6 years

🍷 Complex, subtle nose; smooth, elegant and rounded in the mouth, with a fine balance of fruit

🍴 Meaty pasta dishes, roasted and grilled meats

Moreover, the Institute's own small but well equipped "*cantina sperimentale*" (experimental winery) in Marsala offers students taking a short degree course in Oenology and Viticulture some valuable hands-on experience.

In the early stages of Sicily's wine renaissance, it was oenologists from Piedmont and Tuscany (in some cases, from California, Australia and New Zealand as well) who guided the planting, the pruning, the harvesting, the wine-making and the blending that have helped make Sicilian wines great. Foremost among them has been the great Giacomo Tachis, the doyen of Italian viticulture (creator of legendary Tuscan wines such as *Sassicaia*, *Tignanello* and *Solaia*), whose unflagging enthusiasm and help continue to inspire quality winemakers throughout the island.

Fortunately, to summon outside expertise there was a new generation of local winemakers familiar with winemaking elsewhere and endowed with admirable entrepreneurial spirit. Some of these came from old winemaking families, the enlightened landowners who had always devoted some of their agriculture to grape growing. The Planetas themselves, for example, or the Tasca d'Almerita family at the Regaleali estate, the Rallo family that owns the Donnafugata winery, or Marco De Bartoli who has done so much to renew and refine the image of Marsala.

Alongside such well-established viticultural realities, however, there are also a number of relative newcomers. In Sicily it is not unusual to meet young winemakers who are hardly out of their twenties and are already producing wines of remarkable calibre and elegance. The emergence over the past few years of a steady flow of locally trained wine technicians completes the sensation of renewal.

Enterprising Sicilian winemakers initially saw fit to showcase what their terroir could produce by concentrating on wine genres that were readily recognisable to international wine critics. This accounts for the Syrahs, the Cabernet Sauvignons, the Merlots and the Chardonnays that have gained widespread praise for their rich fruits, good structure and ageing potential.

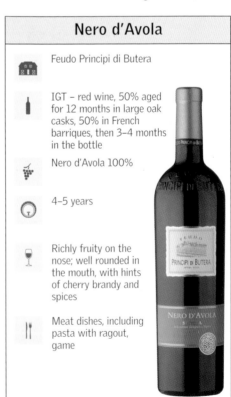

Nero d'Avola

🏠 Feudo Principi di Butera

🍾 IGT – red wine, 50% aged for 12 months in large oak casks, 50% in French barriques, then 3–4 months in the bottle

🍇 Nero d'Avola 100%

🌡 4–5 years

🍷 Richly fruity on the nose; well rounded in the mouth, with hints of cherry brandy and spices

🍴 Meat dishes, including pasta with ragout, game

↻ *New casks made by Marsal Botti, the Marsala-based coopers that is investing the traditional craft with advanced technology to keep abreast of the market and supply quality wineries with barrels of all sizes.*

➲ *Cask for Passito in the historic Bonsulton cellars on the Island of Pantelleria.*

The next stage has been to blend some of these with indigenous grape varieties: Cabernet Sauvignon with Nero d'Avola, for instance; or Chardonnay and Inzolia.

However, the challenge that Sicilian winemakers now find most enticing is the creation of unique quality wines with traditional Sicilian grape varieties. Of these, Nero d'Avola is generally recognized as being the sovereign red grape.

Whereas elsewhere in Italy quality wines have tended to belong to the various DOCs (*Denominazione d'Origine Controllata*, the Italian equivalent of a French Appellation), so far in Sicily this has not been the case. This may be partly because the production norms pertaining to each DOC are perceived as being too restrictive. Arguably it also has to do with a certain independence of spirit: Sicilians, yes; but individuals rather than clan members.

Yet Alessio Planeta, whose family winery has paved the way for change by anticipating forthcoming trends with extraordinary insight and courage, is convinced that in coming years the Sicilian DOCs will be seen by winemakers as an exciting challenge that can give the island's wine production a greater degree of cohesion and identity.

As the future unfurls, which it does with great speed in Sicily, the aim of this book is twofold: to introduce readers to Sicily through the island's foremost ambassador, its wine; and to enrich appreciation of Sicily's wines by describing where they come from and how they are made. Just as Sicilian culture is enormously rich and varied, blending together the ancient Greek, the Phoenician, the Roman, the Arab, the Spanish and the Norman, so its inhabitants are complex and highly individualistic. Little wonder, therefore, that they are able to make wines of great depth and originality.

↷ *Students of oenology and viticulture take the measure of their future art at the experimental winery attached to their Institute in Marsala.*

⮎ *The immaculately planted and tended vinescape at the Regaleali estate, where the provinces of Palermo and Caltanissetta meet.*

⮌ *Once restoration has been completed, this ancient palmento, or wine press, at Nino Pupillo's historic family estate near Siracusa is destined to become the tasting room.*

Innovation and Tradition

Treasuring the Past

A couple of years ago Giambattista Cilia and Giusto Occhipinti filled a number of terracotta urns with fresh must crushed from Nero d'Avola grapes grown at their COS winery just outside Vittoria, in the south-eastern province of Ragusa. With their 450-litre capacity, the larger containers were half embedded in the ground for stability and natural temperature control. Though at the outset urns of different provenance were selected, it was soon discovered that the Spanish products performed better than their Sicilian and Tunisian counterparts. The idea was to see what oenological history had to offer winemaking today.

Archaeological research has revealed that by the early 5th century BC, if not before, commercial wineries were already operating in the vicinity of Agrigento. One in particular was equipped with a vat that could accommodate the content of 1000 amphorae, each of which contained from 20 to 30 litres. From here a system of ducts fed the wine directly into the storage area fitted with 300 pithoi, or clay urns, set into the rock and each able to hold the wine from 100 amphorae.

Cilia and Occhipinti both have a well-honed empirical interest in how things work that probably derives from their early training as architects. Independence of spirit is their trademark, to the extent that they – almost uniquely – largely do without the services of an oenologist and instead base practically all winemaking decisions on their own considerable experience and intuition.

For them, the past is a potential treasure trove, a source that transcends mere inspiration to suggest actual practice. Hence the experiment with the terracotta urns. The must was kept on its lees in these containers for an astoundingly long eight months, monitored through regular tastings. This critical, hands-on approach suggested a slight divergence from Antiquity, where five months or so would elapse between the September harvest and the *Pithoigia* of late February, when the pithoi were opened to celebrate the birth of the new wine. In their contemporary reading of ancient practice, the COS winemakers duly removed the wine from the skins, pressed these and returned the assembled liquids to clean terracotta containers to settle before bottling. As a constant measure of the wine's evolution, in this ongoing experiment they have been able to make comparisons with wine harvested in the same period from the same vineyard, but fermented in steel and matured in barriques. The two products are remarkably different, yet each in its own way balanced and complete: more mineral aromas among the fruit of the urn-wine; softer tannins and a more familiar fullness in its barrique-aged sibling. The belief that true innovation derives from tradition is shared by many Sicilian winemakers. By this they mean that they may still have much to learn from bygone practice, when winemaking lacked the analyses made in today's well-equipped laboratories, but could certainly count on the cumulative knowledge amassed over generations of extended empirical observation.

With the arrival on the scene of home-grown and often home-trained wine technicians, the focus has widened to embrace, or at least reconsider, local winemaking lore as well. The aim is to ensure that Sicilian quality wines maintain their particular identity as expressions of an inimitable terroir.

↻ *Giusto Occhipinti and Giambattista Cilia of the COS winery.*

➲ *The bottle archive at the COS winery.*

↻ *A monument to tradition: the historic press lovingly preserved at the COS winery just outside Vittoria.*

↻↻ *Terracotta urns, semi-interred for temperature control, containing Nero d'Avola at the COS winery.*

This interrelation of the new and the old is evident in the whole question of vine planting and dressing. Good wines can only be made with quality grapes, which are obtained by coercing the vines into producing a limited quantity of premium fruit. To achieve this, new vineyards are planted densely and pruned radically. Gradually the tall, prolific vines grown as a pergola, or a *tendone*, are being uprooted and replaced with close-knit trellised rows that can be pruned short to produce less. Likewise, the sight of sparsely planted vines leisurely embracing fruit trees for support belongs to the world of viticultural archaeology. Though less bucolic to behold, it is the tight geometrical precision of today's newly planted vineyards that offers the greatest promise.

And yet fifty years ago in Sicily one hectare of vineyard would typically contain eight to ten thousand plants, which is a considerably higher density than is generally achieved today. "When all work in the vineyards was done by hand, this was possible. But with the need to let tractors in between the rows even quality winemakers found themselves reducing density", explains biologist turned oenologist Maria Nicolosi of the Villagrande winery on Mount Etna. "Add to this Sicily's post-war emphasis on quantity, and you get to the point where a hundred quintals (10,000 kilos) of grapes were being forced out of no more than a thousand plants in any given hectare. That meant a massive 10 kilos a plant. No wonder the quality suffered."

At Villagrande current vine-density is typically between 4000 and 4500 plants per hectare, with an average yield of 2.5 kilos of grapes per plant. However, since Maria's son Marco has completed his studies in oenology and viticulture and joined the winery the ratio is increasing to 7500, at his instigation, plus a tractor that is small and versatile enough to work between the rows.

Newly trained and anxious to explore what the past has to offer, Marco gets on well with his oenologist father Carlo, who quietly reins in any youthful excess of experimental zeal. Marco is also keen to see why past generations of Etna winemakers, who had

↑ *Densely planted, trellis-trained vineyards at the Baglio di Pianetto winery at Santa Cristina Gela, due south of Palermo.*

↪ *The early spring landscape typical of the area inland from Agrigento: traditional vinedressing with lower plant density and a pergola training system produces greater quantities of fruit, but of poor quality.*

plentiful oak as well as chestnut to hand, chose to ferment their Nerello Mascalese, the indigenous local red grape variety, in chestnut vats. Elsewhere oak was generally preferred, and is certainly the wood chosen by those winemakers who have retained or returned to wooden vats for fermentation of part of their wines, both reds and whites.

For its own *Etna Rosso DOC*, the Murgo winery, another of the foremost quality producers of the Etna area, opts for an 85/15% marriage of Nerello Mascalese and Nerello Mantellato (also called Nerello Cappuccio) that is largely fermented in steel, then finished for 6 months in large old wooden casks before being blended and bottled. "Here the wood really only serves for oxygenating the wine", explains Michele Scammacca del Murgo. "The point for us is that Nerello Mascalese was traditionally made as a light wine to be drunk young. In fact it naturally lent itself to rosés, and we actually make a fine champagne-style Spumante from it, our *Murgo Brut*. As far as reds are concerned, the market now demands wines of greater body and colour. To achieve this we tend to harvest the Nerello a bit later and use modern wine-making techniques, including selected yeasts and temperature-controlled fermentation, to help it develop the desired muscle". The *Murgo Etna Rosso DOC* is a warm, moderately tannic red with just the right amount of fruit and mineral undertones to provide a discreet accompaniment to white meats.

↻ *The historic cellars at the Barone di Villagrande winery on Mount Etna.*

Timely Solutions

Advanced cooling technology is, as one might expect, the most evident form of innovation found in Sicilian wineries. For white wines in particular, and especially in lower lying coastal areas where the temperatures are higher during the day and don't fall much at night, reasonable longevity and interesting structure owe much to extended fermentation, which is achieved by lowering the temperature of the must.

The Baglio Hopps winery, for instance, located between Marsala and Salemi, just inland from the west coast, has shown that cooling technology can hugely enhance some interesting and hitherto largely unrecognised properties intrinsic to the local Grillo white grape variety: fine aromas, great structure, potential for ageing.

Nino Galfano, the locally raised and trained oenologist, leaves the must on its skins for up to 48 hours (12 hours is probably the average for most whites) at a temperature of 5°C. This is then pressed and the liquid stocked in steel for 24 to 48 hours at a temperature that is low enough to inhibit fermentation. During this time the must will precipitate and clarify, after which it can be transferred to wooden casks for fermentation that lasts, thanks to the temperature control, for as long as 50 to 60 days. Compared with traditional practice, this is remarkably protracted. Together with barrel ageing, it is also what accounts for the flavour and length of the finished product.

The growth of interest in wooden barrels and casks as well as the fashionable smaller French barriques has given a new lease of life to what used to be a flourishing industry in Marsala. Fifty years ago, Marsal Botti was one of the 30 or so coopers supplying barrels to the city's famous fortified wine producers (the top-end *Marsala Vergine Riserva* must be aged in wood for at least 10 years; the other Marsalas for 1, 2, 4 or 5 years, according to genre). With an annual production of around 30,000 barrels, today it is the sole survivor, and with its technologically advanced new factory it is gradually expanding.

↻ *Rescued and refurbished, the concrete vats at the Ceuso winery near Alcamo are considered the ideal containers for maturing wines.*

➲ *Opposite page, master cooper Giuseppe Li Causi at work.*

➲➲ *Large casks nearing completion at the Marsal Botti workshop in Marsala.*

Girolamo Li Causi, who learnt the art of traditional cooperage from his father Giuseppe, makes frequent visits to France, where he selects the oak that, duly seasoned, will arrive in planks of the right length for the various sized barrels the company makes. In coming years he feels that Romania and Hungary could also become suppliers of the raw material.

"We are specialised in 450 litre casks, which are ideal for Sicilian wines", explains Girolamo. "In fact we have even had requests for collaboration from French coopers for this sized product. Our range goes from the highly computerised production of barriques that we manufacture in the new factory with its sophisticated French equipment, to the large barrels with a 1000 litre capacity, or more, which are produced entirely by hand in the old, traditional workshop down near the port".

Although temperature controlled steel vats are found in practically all quality wineries, recently the fibreglass resin-lined concrete vats of the 1950s and 60s have been making a timid comeback. It is

suggested that matured or maturing wines can be upset by the slight electromagnetic build-up possible in steel, but impossible in totally inert concrete. So the huge rectangular containers that escaped destruction when steel was held to be the quintessence of oenological modernity are now being restored, repainted and regarded as a boon rather than a waste of space.

At his family wine estate set among the beautiful rolling hills between Alcamo and Camporeale, in the province of Palermo, Francesco Spadafora is gradually restoring the old concrete wine vats and making a colourful feature of the same material for the houses that surround the farmyard. Likewise the three Melia brothers at the Ceuso winery, just the other side of Alcamo, have brought new life to the concrete containers long since installed in the baglio, or fortified farm building, that has recently become their headquarters.

As Sicily's foremost expert in viticulture, Vincenzo Melia is now much in demand as a consultant for new plantings elsewhere in Italy. He is also the most senior technician at the Regional Institute for Viticulture and

Wine, and thus more than most aware of the goals and achievements of other wineries. "Wines matured in concrete vats precipitate perfectly. Moreover, they are protected from drastic temperature changes. We don't filter our wines. As the great Giacomo Tachis has pointed out, filtering wines removes the larger particles, which are the proteins. With these gone the wine is no longer able to evolve".

Not filtering constitutes a return to tradition that has a growing number of aficionados. Marco Nicolosi is one of the young winemakers who look forward to acting on their conviction that colour, aromas and flavour are lost during the break-up of microelements that comes about with filtering. Though others claim that these are largely reconstituted as the filtered wine settles, Nicolosi hopes in future years that the Villagrande reds will be unfiltered.

Giambattista Cilia of the COS winery believes that tradition suggests additional ways of ensuring a wine's stability and clarity in the bottle. "We pay great attention to the phases of the moon", he declares. "We like to prune when there is no moon; and we bottle

Advanced cooling technology: Cantine Settesoli at Menfi (left), in the Province of Agrigento; Baglio di Pianetto at Santa Cristina Gela (above), in the Province of Palermo.

when the moon is new, since a full moon tends to make elements rise. If you think what it does to tides, you can imagine it would also influence the constituent parts of wine".

The COS winemakers go several steps further in their return to tradition in pursuit of distinctive wines. For fermentation most wineries use yeasts that are specially selected to perform as required in particular conditions. It is a question of expedience. Certain yeast cultures are developed to withstand high temperatures, for instance; others to complete their life cycle before all the sugars have been transformed into alcohol, which is fundamental in the production of raisin wines where a residual sweetness is an essential part of the finished product.

Airborne yeasts are naturally present in and around wineries, however, and it is these that Cilia and Occhipinti have opted to use. "We used select cultured yeasts for two years, and we simply couldn't recognise our wines", explains Cilia. "They were technically perfect, but they could have come from anywhere. To use ambient yeasts we have to be extra careful about quality control in the vineyard. The pickers are told to harvest only what they would put in their own mouths, we collect the bunches in shallow boxes so that no uncontrolled processes get under way in the lower layers, and once the grapes are at the winery we have women, who are much more picky, surveying the conveyance belt and removing anything less than perfect before the crushing process begins. Like this we obtain select natural yeasts".

Other wineries have adopted ad-hoc low-grade innovations that simply improve a tried and tested system. With appropriate lighting, in some cases provided by photovoltaic energy, it is now possible to harvest at night, when the temperatures are lower and the grapes less prone to ferment en route to the winery. The first winery to do this was Donnafugata at its Contessa Entellina vineyards in the Belice Valley, on the west side of the island. The operation has paid off in terms of image as well. Though it may be commonplace in Australia, the practice is so far removed from

➲ *Grape harvesting at night at Contessa Entellina at the Donnafugata Estate.*

traditional Italian custom that it has stuck in the public imagination more strongly than the most efficacious advertising campaign.

On the volcanic island of Pantelleria, to the extreme south west of Sicily's western coast, Donnafugata also produces an excellent raisin wine, the *Ben Ryé*, made from the local Zibibbo grapes, also known as Muscat of Alexandria. So strong are the winds that pummel the island most of the year that only plants surrounded by walls can hope to achieve any height. In the case of the vines, they are grown in concave depressions in the ground, and so pruned as to extend horizontally rather than vertically. In winter, when they are dormant and without foliage, they resemble the mandrakes of medieval herbals.

In such conditions, the newly planted vines on the terraced hillsides take time to get established. To help them withstand the stress of the elements, the Donnafugata vinedressers have recently introduced a simple, low-technology contrivance that was once commonplace in the coastal vineyards of Marsala, where most of these workers come from: a windbreak made of feathery canes

deeply embedded in the soil and reinforced by means of horizontal elements of the same material.

As they set to work in blustery winter weather constructing this shield, the Marsalese labourers attracted a constant flow of curious locals, who stopped to gaze in disbelief and then expressed their conviction that the whole lot would fly away with the first serious gusts. Six months later the gently swaying windbreaks were still standing, just as intended, and the newly planted vines were doing just fine.

Several years ago, much the same attitude greeted another small, low-key innovation introduced by the same people. Some of the grapes harvested for the lush, apricot-nosed Moscato Passito di Pantelleria are picked fully ripe. The rest must be dried out in the sun for as much as 30 days before they are crushed. Traditionally these grapes were laid outdoors on mounds of dried grasses, and nowadays more commonly on cane trays.

Since the bunches are compact and the individual grapes larger than their Moscato cousins grown around Noto and the Malvasia from the

⊃ *Frappato grapes near Vittoria, almost ready for havesting.*

⊃ *At the Donnafugata winery on Pantelleria, Zibibbo grapes layed out on trays that can be conveniently turned each day during the drying process.*

island of Salina, they need to be turned from time to time to make sure the dry air reaches all sides of the fruit. Carefully turning individual bunches is of course labour intensive. However, much time and effort can be saved by turning over whole trays, duly adjusted in their design so that they can be stood one on another and then turned upside down. This small improvement has now become widespread. It will be interesting to see whether, in future years, the windbreaks also find such favour.

When it comes to where and what grapes are planted, in Sicily tradition and innovation are somewhat relative categories. There are certain areas of the island where vines have been cultivated since time immemorial. Records dating back to the 5th century BC mention both the sweet Pollios wine of Siracusa and the commercial wine production of Agrigento, in the south west. Morgantina in central Sicily, Taormina on the south east coast and the Etna area were also renowned for their wines in Antiquity.

In early modern times, other areas came to the fore. During the nineteenth century, the wines made from the local Nero d'Avola grapes at Pachino and Vittoria in the southeast were much appreciated by French wine merchants for their ability to give body to products from the Gironde and Burgundy. By the 1860s, viticulture was most widespread in the provinces of Palermo, Trapani and Catania, with the province of Trapani playing a leading role twenty years later.

Then, between the end of the 1800s and the beginning of the 1900s, the outbreak of phylloxera that had already destroyed mainland European viticulture reached Sicily and wrought immense damage. Not only was the subsequent replanting insufficient to cover the hectares lost, but pest-resistant American rootstock had to be used for grafting, and many local grape varieties came in for a protracted period of neglect.

In the post-war period, before Sicily's wine renaissance got under way, it was the most prolific grape varieties that enjoyed greatest favour. These included "imported" Italian varieties such as the white

Trebbiano grape grown extensively in central Italy. By the 1990s, with the new focus on quality, planting French grape varieties such as Cabernet Sauvignon, Merlot, Syrah and Chardonnay appeared to be a form of innovation. Today this has become almost the norm, and it is the search for distinctive Sicilian wines made from the many native grape varieties that has the aura of cutting edge.

Long before wines came to be conjugated with fashions, however, the Tasca d'Almerita winery was engaged in finding out just what did well where, and in what kinds of soil. At the family's Tenuta di Regaleali, located between Vallelunga in the province of Caltanissetta and Valledolmo in the province of Palermo, considerable space and resources have long been devoted to ongoing research. Experiments with 80 varieties of vine, both local and of far-flung origin, have enormously facilitated the island's current focus on quality wine production.

Greater space will be devoted to the coexistence of native and imported grape varieties and the rewards of their interaction in the next chapter, which will also focus on the somewhat confusing universe of the Sicilian DOCs, or appellations, and their geographical extension. For the present, it is perhaps worth pointing out that although certain areas of Sicily may seem to lack any vocation for viticulture, even this is a concept that calls for constant revision.

Just as the western part of the island, which now produces some fine table wines, was largely devoted to cereal and pulse farming until the 1970s, so other areas are being discovered, or rediscovered, and converted to viticulture with remarkable results. One case in point is the large Abbazia Santa Anastasia estate located near Castelbuono, just inland from Cefalù and slightly east of Palermo. At the centre of the property is what was once an important Benedictine monastery, now a fine hotel. Founded in 1100, in centuries past the monastery is said to have produced a wine that was admired as far afield as Rome. However, there had been no significant viticulture at Castelbuono within in living memory when Francesco Lena purchased the property in 1980 and began planting

⊃ The courtyard at Abbazia Sant Anastasia, near Castelbuono. The buildings that once housed the monks have been turned into a luxury hotel, located right in the middle of the wine estate.

⊃ Vines flourishing at Tenuta di Budonetto, Francesco Maurigi's estate near Piazza Armerina.

vines, both Sicilian and French, under the guidance of Vincenzo Melia, among others, from the Regional Institute for Viticulture and Wine. The first bottles appeared on the market in the early 1990s, and since then have met with acclaim both within Sicily and abroad. Lena had the foresight and persistence to recreate, in contemporary terms, what had been lost in time. Even greater intuition, conviction and individualism are required to plant vines where viticulture has never existed. This is what Francesco Maurigi has done at the Tenuta di Budonetto, just a short distance from the famous Roman Villa del Casale at Piazza Armerina, towards the centre of the island. Major landowners, his family had extensive properties in central and western Sicily, some of which Francesco sold to buy the land and dilapidated farmhouse on which he had set his heart. The house was duly restored, and vines were planted in 1998, with an exclusive preference for French grape varieties, the only ones, in his view, "capable of producing great wines". Though his consultant oenologist told him to resist the temptation to make

wine with his first vintage in 2000, he proceeded nevertheless, with a certain degree of guesswork, in order to find out what his chosen terroir could produce. The resultant 6000 bottles were more than encouraging, and two years later he had his own stand at Vinitaly and all four wines in the Wine Spectator. The characteristic they share is elegance, a significant achievement for an area traditionally held to be insignificant for viticulture. It goes without saying that other winemakers are now eyeing the area with due interest.

The point is, of course, that the wine map of Sicily is no static entity. Its essential dynamism is partly due to the constant interaction of past and present that is typical of Sicilian culture in general; partly to the forward-looking entrepreneurial spirit of winemakers who are inspired, but not hidebound, by their island's many-faceted history. If individualism is the byword, it is not of the invidious variety. Instead, each producer is like a colourful tessera in a mosaic whose outline coincides with that of the island.

➲ *Francesco Maurigi, who had the vision and courage to plant vines near Piazza Armerina, where there had hitherto been no tradition of viticulture.*

➲ *View of the Tenuta di Budonetto Estate near Piazza Armerina.*

Grape Varieties and Appellations

Outlining the Wine Map

For the present, to use the Denominations of Controlled Origin, or DOCs, as a key to Sicily's wine map can be a little frustrating. For whereas the mere mention of other Italian regions conjures up images of well established appellations (Barolo, Barbaresco, Barbera in Piedmont; Chianti, Vino Nobile di Montepulciano, Brunello di Montalcino in Tuscany), in Sicily very few of the 19 different appellations actually mean anything to wine drinkers outside the specific growing areas. Indeed, there are several Sicilian DOCs that are of little more than formal significance even within their own proclaimed districts. Yet though they may have been set up at the behest of some local dignitary with a keener nose for political expedience than viticultural reality, the chances are that within a few years producers of fine wines will choose to use these appellations as a collective way of obtaining recognition for a specific area of what is, unquestionably, a large and varied island.

In the early day's of Sicily's wine renaissance, many independent-minded producers preferred to make and market their wines as IGTs, which gave them greater freedom when it came to blends and

Indigenous Sicilian Grape Varieties

REDS

Nero d'Avola
Also known as Calabrese, and thought to be Sicily's most promising red. First grown many centuries ago around Avola, and then Noto and Pachino, in the province of Siracusa, it is now widely grown throughout the island, except on Etna. It forms the backbone of Eloro DOC and Cerasuolo di Vittoria DOC, as well as several of the newer appellations such as the Contea di Sclafani, Contessa Entellina and Monreale DOCs. Produces wines of rich, fruity structure that lend themselves to ageing.

Nerello Mascalese
The main indigenous grape variety of Mount Etna, constituting at least 80% of Etna Rosso DOC. Grown from altitudes of 350 to 1000 metres, this late-ripening grape produces wines that age well, with pleasant tannins and interesting spicy aromas that vary in relation to the exact growing area.

Nerello Cappuccio
The other indigenous red grape from Mount Etna, constituting up to 20% of the blend in the Etna Rosso DOC. Also called Nerello Mantellato on account of the cape-like way it hangs down from the vine trained in the traditional alberello fashion. It tends to ripen between late September and early October, well in advance of its Etnean counterpart, the Nerello Mascalese, producing on its own wines to be drunk relatively young.

Frappato di Vittoria
Grown at least since the 17th century around Vittoria, in the south-eastern province of Ragusa. Must constitute at least 40% of the blend in Cerasuolo di Vittorio DOC, where it marries its cherry-light aromas and fresh elegance with the fruit and structure of Nero d'Avola.

Perricone
Also known as Pignatello, between the end of the 1800s and the beginning of the 1900s, this grape variety was widespread in the provinces of Trapani and Palermo. Following decades of neglect, it is slowly returning in blends such as the Contea di Sclafani, the Eloro and the Delia Nivolelli appellation, and hopefully also in coming years as a promising single varietal.

Nocera
Variety native to the Messina area that was once widely grown and has now become rare, despite its inclusion in the Faro DOC. During the mid-19th century, Nocera was exported to the Provence and Beaujolais areas of France, where it was known as Suquet and Barbe du Sultan. Duly ripened, the grape combines sweetness with good acidity.

WHITES

Catarratto
The most widespread native white grape variety in Sicily, and the second most widespread in Italy after Trebbiano. The variety comprises at least two major clones ("comune" and the slightly waxy "lucido serrato"), and a number of sub-clones whose characteristics vary considerably. While once used almost exclusively for Marsala, thanks to modern winemaking techniques Catarratto is now widely used in the table wine blends defined by the Contessa Entellina, the Contea di Sclafani, the Etna, the Alcamo and the Monreale DOCs. It is also emerging as an interesting varietal in its own right.

Inzolia
Also known as Ansonica, it is grown widely in the provinces of Agrigento, Palermo and Caltanisetta. Fully ripe, these golden yellow grapes are rich in sugars, but low in acidity. To make the fine single-variety table wines for which Sicily is gaining renown, this grape needs to be picked slightly before it is fully ripe.

Grillo
Widespread in western Sicily by the late 1800s, this grape variety was originally cultivated as a component part of Marsala. Because the yields tend to be low, by the 1960s it had largely been uprooted and replaced by Catarratto. Today it accounts for a mere 3% of vinegrowing in the Trapani area. It is now used to create some fine single-variety wines that maintain their characteristic freshness and elegance for some time, as well as featuring as a blend in DOCs such as Monreale, Alcamo and Contea di Sclafani.

Grecanico
Grown largely in western Sicily, though for the present not in great quantity, this variety produces long, somewhat straggly bunches of grapes that can be made into wines of fine flavour, elegance and balance. It is thus often used in blended whites, featuring in several of the DOCs of western Sicily, particularly around Menfi. Though Grecanico tends to be the lesser marriage partner, in Planeta's excellent *La Segreta Bianco IGT*, it accounts for 60% of the blend.

Damaschino
Although this is the most productive Sicilian grape variety, its cultivation is not widespread because the plant's natural exuberance easily leads to the growth of infertile shoots. Moreover, the grapes themselves are more subject than other varieties to rot. To add to this, sugar content and acidity both tend to be low. That said, when duly tended Damaschino can produce simple, light wines to be enjoyed young. A rare and persuasive example of the genre is Centonze's *Luce e Colori Bianco IGT*. Donnafugata also produces a Damaschino varietal, the *Damaskino Bianco IGT*.

Albanello
Grown in very limited quantities in the provinces of Ragusa and Siracusa, the thick-skinned grapes of this variety turn golden where they face the sun. The current lack of commercially available wines made with this variety undermines for the present the claim that it lends itself to the production of fine whites that accompany fish well. However, the fact that the Planeta vineyards at Noto include a little Albanello suggests that perhaps in future the variety may emerge from oblivion.

Carricante
This very ancient grape variety is indigenous to Mount Etna, where it is part of the Etna Bianco DOCs. Like all the Etna varieties, it ripens late, and produces wines of high acidity for which malolactic fermentation is essential. If properly cultivated and vinified, it can produce great white wines of remarkably longevity (10 years or more) that preserve their aromas of apple, orange blossom and anice without sacrificing the acidic freshness from which their structure derives.

Minnella
Found in the older vineyards of Mount Etna, it ripens in late September, a couple of weeks earlier than the other Etna varieties. Its name derives from the word minna, a dialectal term for breast, suggesting the slightly elongated shape of the grape. It may account for up to 10% of the Etna DOC blend, but has so far only been used for a single variety wine by Benanti, who has produced a limited quantity of an interesting white wine with rich, ripe fruity aromas, a slight hint of anice and a long, dry finish.

Moscato
The Muscat grapes grown in Sicily for dessert wines are all white. They include the honey-sweet Moscato bianco di Siracusa, recently revived by the Pupillo winery, and the Moscato bianco di Noto, which is currently being rescued from oblivion by the Planeta winery. Although they two grapes belong to the same variety, the wines they produce are bound to differ on account of the differences in altitude, microclimate and soil between the hilly area around Noto and the flatter terroir of coastal Siracusa. Related to this grape is the Moscato di Alessandria, also known as Zibibbo, grown on the island of Pantelleria to make raisin wine. This has larger, highly aromatic grapes that grow in more compact bunches and ripen between late July and mid September.

Malvasia
Cultivated in particular on the island of Salina, in the Aeolian archipelago, this smallish, aromatic grape grows in straggly bunches and is dried to make Malvasia delle Lipari, a sumptuous, peachy raisin wine.

Stromboli

AEOLIAN ISLANDS

Filicudi
Panarea
Alicudi
Salina
Lipari
Vulcano

THYRRHENIAN SEA

Messina

PALERMO ●

Trapani ●

IONIAN
SEA

● Enna

● Catania

Caltanissetta ●

● Agrigento

Siracusa ●

MEDITERRANEAN SEA

Ragusa ●

Pantelleria

The DOCs

	Alcamo or Bianco d'Alcamo
	Cerasuolo di Vittoria
	Contea di Sclafani
	Contessa Entellina
	Delia Nivolelli

	Eloro
	Etna
	Faro
	Malvasia delle Lipari
	Marsala
	Menfi
	Monreale

	Moscato di Noto Naturale
	Moscato di Pantelleria Naturale or Passito
	Moscato di Siracusa
	Riesi
	Sambuca di Sicilia
	Santa Margherita di Belice
	Sciacca

ageing. The reason for this is that the Indicazione Geografica Tipica simply and solely suggests that the given wine is a true expression of the terroir in which it is made.

However, as more and more producers turn to quality, the proliferation of IGTs is bound to dilute the winemaker's chance of establishing for his best wines a recognisable identity. In other words, surrounded by a giddy ocean of different IGTs, the consumer may find it hard to remember the name of a particular producer. Conversely, he or she is more likely to recall the name of a DOC, and from here find it easier to trace the name once read on a label.

The Recognisable DOCs

There are currently nine Sicilian DOCs whose renown has spread beyond the island's shores. Unquestionably the foremost is the Cerasuolo di Vittoria, which in coming months is also likely to become the first of the island's DOCGs, the super category of appellations that are both "controllata" and "garantita".

Cerasuolo di Vittoria is produced in and around the town of Vittoria, not far from Ragusa in southeastern Sicily. The name itself suggests the light, bright fruitiness of cherries, which is the characteristic of the local Frappato grape variety that accounts for at least 40% of the blend. The remaining 60% is generally made up of Nero d'Avola, also known as Calabrese, the imposing red grape variety that originates in this southern tip of Sicily, though 10% of Nerello Mascalese, the Etna red, may also be included.

The art of the Cerasuolo di Vittoria is to produce a wine that does not sacrifice the fresh fruitiness of the Frappato on the altar of structure and longevity. It is a fine balance, because of course good structure is essential for the wine's continued evolution.

A number of wineries, including COS, Avide and Poggio di Bortolone, make more than one Cerasuolo, varying the ratio of Frappato and Nero d'Avola to obtain more or less fresh, slightly raspberry-like fruit.

↥ *Thoughtful planting at the Contrada Fontane estate belonging to the COS winery run by Giusto Occhipinti and Giambattista Cilia.*

↺ *Domenico Buffa, a passionate upholder of quality Marsala.*

For its intriguing *Vastunaca Cerasuolo di Vittoria*, the COS winery uses 80% Frappato and 20% Nero d'Avola, ageing the wine in steel for 9 to 12 months. Light, ruby red in colour, the Poggio di Bortolone *Contessa Costanza Cerasuolo* is a 50/50 blend that imbues plenty of clear, fruity aromas with a hint of tobacco. By contrast, the Valle dell'Acate winery makes just the one classic blend, ageing the 60% Nero d'Avola component in barriques for 8 to 9 months to create a wine of great elegance and a certain international flair. "We opted to do this because we also produce *Il Frappato*, which is my father's proud creation, an IGT made entirely with the Frappato grape variety", explains Gaetana Jacono, business manager of the family winery. "It isn't easy to obtain the lovely light fruitiness and depth of colour we've achieved with Frappato grapes. We macerated the must on the skins for 10 days at a low temperature before fermentation to draw out the aromas". Designed for early drinking, this berry-ripe wine is an affectionate tribute to the airy, vine-clad valley from which it derives.

Second of the Sicilian DOCs in terms of international renown is undoubtedly Marsala, if only because the name brings with it unfortunate connotations of sickly sweet cooking wines. Discovered and promoted by John Woodhouse, an English businessman who visited Sicily in 1770, the excellent fortified wine made near the western port town of Marsala enjoyed considerable international fame until the 1960s, when quality became erratic and the image of the product suffered a decline.

As a reaction, Marco De Bartoli, the foremost of the quality producers in the area, refuses to use the word "Marsala" for his magnificent dessert wine, instead calling it *Vecchio Samperi*. This he makes not with the addition of alcohol, as countenanced by the regulations, but by means of the traditional Solera method in which small quantities of young wines are added to wines of older vintages as they pass through a sequence of wooden barrels.

Happily, De Bartoli is now no longer entirely isolated in his pursuit of a product to be proud of. Indeed, a good *Marsala*

Barocco	Vecchio Samperi Ventennale	Marsala Vergine
Avide	Marco De Bartoli	Buffa
Cerasuolo di Vittoria DOC – red wine aged for 8 months in barriques and a further 18-24 months in the bottle	White wine aged for 12 months in chestnut casks, then "fortified" over twenty years in oak with the Solera method of fractional blending of younger with more mature barrel batches	Marsala DOC – fortified white wine aged for at least five years in Slavonian oak followed by French oak
Frappato 60%, Nero d'Avola 40%	Grillo 100%	Grillo 100%
2-3 years	15 years at least	Evolves continuously with ageing
Fresh and fruity on the nose; dry and full bodied in the mouth, with pleasant tannins and a slightly bitter finish	Aromas of raisins and almond paste; clean and perfectly balanced in the mouth, with a persistent note of toast and spice	Raisins, fruit, caramel, vanilla and later almonds on the nose; dry yet fruity and smooth in the mouth
Rabbit, hare and chicken dishes, cheese pasta timbale, pasta with tasty vegetable sauces	Nutty dry biscuits, simple sponge cake, mature hard cheese	Seasoned cheeses, almond biscuits, chocolate

Vergine DOC such as the one produced by Buffa, under the enlightened direction of chemist turned oenologist Domenico Buffa, can be smooth, dry, nutty and full of character. Made from Grillo grapes fortified with the "mistella" alcohol derived from must and aqua vitae, the *Buffa Marsala Vergine* is aged for five years in wood and accompanies both chocolate and mature cheeses extraordinarily well.

The white grape varieties typically grown in and around Marsala are Grillo, Catarratto and Inzolia (often called Ansonica in this part of the island), all of which are indigenous to Sicily. Along with native reds such as Pignatello (elsewhere on the island known as Perricone), Nerello Mascalese and Nero d'Avola, in different combinations they form the essence of all Marsalas and until recently were grown almost exclusively for this purpose.

One of the interesting developments of current Sicilian winemaking over on the west coast has been to focus selectively on these grapes to make some superior table wines, especially whites.

Marco De Bartoli's *Grappoli del Grillo*, the Baglio Hopps *Grillo*, the *Duca di Castelmonte Grillo* and the Cantine Rallo *Gruali*, all of which are IGTs, stand out as excellent cases in point.

While the area down by the coast favour the process of oxidization, which is desirable for Marsala, this is not good for table wines. The Marsala-based Cantine Rallo winery, which produces around 2 million bottles a year, has recently shifted its main focus from Marsala to table wines. For their whites, the chosen growing area is just inland and a little higher up, between Salemi and Palermo.

Part of this area falls within the confines of the Alcamo DOC, a white wine appellation based on the indigenous Catarratto, plus up to 20% of two other indigenous whites, Grecanico and Damaschino, or the same percentage of the Trebbiano variety that was introduced from the mainland during the 1960s on account of its abundant yields. For the moment, Alcamo DOC is largely equated with an enormous output of rather ordinary table wines and just a few quality producers.

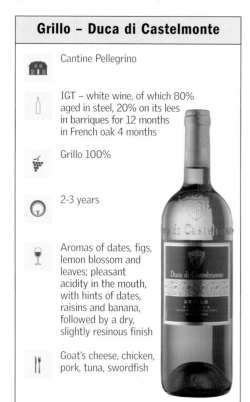

Grillo – Duca di Castelmonte

Cantine Pellegrino

IGT – white wine, of which 80% aged in steel, 20% on its lees in barriques for 12 months in French oak 4 months

Grillo 100%

2-3 years

Aromas of dates, figs, lemon blossom and leaves; pleasant acidity in the mouth, with hints of dates, raisins and banana, followed by a dry, slightly resinous finish

Goat's cheese, chicken, pork, tuna, swordfish

⌂ Overlooking the Principi di Spadafora estate at Contrada Virzì, in the Monreale DOC area south west of Palermo.

⮑ The cellars at the Tasca d'Almerita family's Regaleali estate near Vallelunga, south east of Palermo.

One of these is unquestionably Cantine Rallo, whose reasonably priced *Carta D'oro Alcamo DOC* is made with the shiny-coated "extralucido" clone of Catarratto that produces a wine free of the slightly bitter aftertaste often associated with its more widespread sibling. Indeed, the Gold Medal winning *Carta D'Oro 2001* had a lovely bouquet of spring flowers and ripe cut grass, plus great balance, length and depth of taste, including aromas of ripe banana. Another interesting producer to place a small bet on the Alcamo appellation is Cusumano, located at Partinico, closer to Palermo. Their only concession to DOCs within a fairly wide range of IGTs is their fresh, somewhat citrusy *Nadaria Alcamo Bianco DOC*, made exclusively from Inzolia grapes. The *Principe di Corleone Bianco Alcamo DOC* made by the Pollara winery also stands out as a quality product amid a sea of more commercial wines.

The fact that Alcamo DOC still tends to conjure up images of supermarket shelves has encouraged a number of quality producers within that district to opt instead for the neighbouring and relatively new Monreale DOC, positioned between the town of Alcamo and Palermo. Founded in 2000, this appellation embraces rosés and reds as well as white wines, including single-variety whites and reds made with Sicilian (Inzolia, Catarratto and Grillo for the whites; Nero d'Avola and Perricone for the reds), mainland Italian (Pinot Bianco for the whites; Pinot Nero and Sangiovese for the reds) and international grape varieties (Chardonnay for the whites; Cabernet Sauvignon, Syrah and Merlot for the reds).

The Monreale DOC is so young that it has hardly had time to establish its own identity. However, with producers of the calibre of Francesco Spadafora lending it credence, it will certainly be an appellation to watch in coming years. The Spadafora *Alhambra Monreale Bianco DOC* is a fresh, slightly fruity, dry blend of Catarratto and Inzolia that is well suited to accompany fish. Another winery that has embraced the Monreale appellation is the small partnership of organic growers who have come together under the

Carta d'Oro

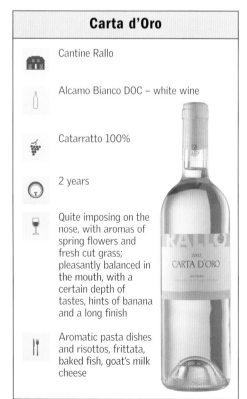

Cantine Rallo

Alcamo Bianco DOC – white wine

Catarratto 100%

2 years

Quite imposing on the nose, with aromas of spring flowers and fresh cut grass; pleasantly balanced in the mouth, with a certain depth of tastes, hints of banana and a long finish

Aromatic pasta dishes and risottos, frittata, baked fish, goat's milk cheese

Rosso del Conte

Tasca d'Almerita

Contea di Sclafani DOC – red wine aged for 12 months in barriques

Nero d'Avola 97%, Perricone 3%

At least 15 years; 30 in ideal conditions

Berries, spice and tobacco in abundance on the nose; plenty of ripe fruit in the mouth, persistent soft tannins and a hint of resin in the finish

Red meats, game, meaty stews

↺ *Vineyards at the Regaleali estate belonging to the Tasca d'Almerita family.*

➲ *View of the Barone di Villagrande vineyards near Milo on Mount Etna.*

label Feotto dello Jato, based on the hillsides around the San Giuseppe Jato, about 24 kilometres south of Palermo.

Due east and inland from the Alcamo appellation area is the well established Contea di Sclafani DOC, whose renown owes much to large, internationally recognised wineries such as Tasca d'Almerita at their Regaleali Estate, positioned between 400 and 750 metres above sea level and surrounded by landscapes of consummate beauty. The Tasca family was one of the first in Sicily to introduce short pruning with the aim of obtaining low yields of premium grapes; likewise it paved the way for others by foreseeing the potential of the indigenous Inzolia and Nero d'Avola grape varieties.

Like its younger Monreale counterpart, the Contea di Sclafani appellation comprises a very catholic range of reds, whites and a rosé. The reds and whites can be made as blends of indigenous grape varieties (respectively, Nero d'Avola and Perricone; Catarratto, Inzolia and Grecanico), or as single variety wines made with much the same range of local and international grapes.

The other Sicilian appellation that has reached consumers far afield is Contessa Entellina DOC, which comprises single variety and blended whites and reds, with an emphasis on international varieties for the latter. Located due south of the Alcamo DOC in the further reaches of the Belice valley, at the heart of western Sicily, the relatively small growing zone owes its fame exclusively to one winery: Donnafugata, a established family concern with a well orchestrated international profile. The five different Contessa Entellina DOC wines made by Donnafugata are all reliably good.

The western side of Sicily is also famous for dessert wine: the Passito di Pantelleria DOC made with Zibibbo grapes grown and sun dried on the windswept volcanic island of Pantelleria, a blustery ferry ride south west of the coast. The Donnafugata *Ben Ryé*, apricot sweet and with a curiously dry finish, is a fine example of this genre. So is the Miceli *Nun Moscato Passito DOC*. The same company also produces a Pantelleria Bianco DOC called *Yrnm*, a

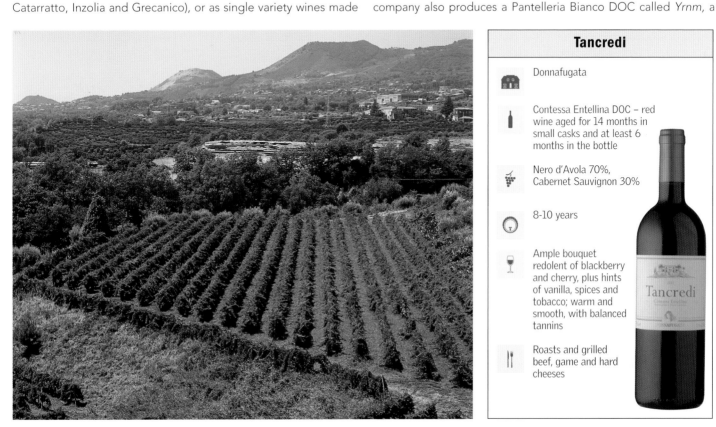

Tancredi

Donnafugata

Contessa Entellina DOC – red wine aged for 14 months in small casks and at least 6 months in the bottle

Nero d'Avola 70%, Cabernet Sauvignon 30%

8-10 years

Ample bouquet redolent of blackberry and cherry, plus hints of vanilla, spices and tobacco; warm and smooth, with balanced tannins

Roasts and grilled beef, game and hard cheeses

thoroughly seductive dry white made with Zibibbo grapes. Salvatore Murana's much-acclaimed *Moscato Passito di Pantelleria Martingana* also deserves the many praises is receives. But arguably the most authentic products are those produced by Marco De Bartoli at his Bukkuram winery and Roberto Casano at the Bonsulton winery. Both ensure that the carefully selected grapes laid out on the grassy ground to dry in the sun are hand turned each day, which is a considerable undertaking even for the youthful limbs of De Bartoli's sons.

The two remaining Sicilian appellations that stand out in their own right owe this distinction to very particular grape varieties and an extraordinary geological context. One is the Malvasia delle Lipari DOC, an apricot-tinged, sun-drenched raisin wine made with Malvasia grapes on the tiny volcanic island of Salina, which is part of the Eolian archipelago situated in the Tyrrhenian sea, off the north coast of Sicily. The other is the time-honoured Etna DOC made on the terraced slopes of the volcano. This consists of a red made with the local Nerello Mascalese and Nerello Cappuccio (or Mantellato) in ratios of 80% and 20% respectively, and a white largely based on the indigenous Carricante grape variety whose characteristic asperity can be tempered with up to 40% Catarratto, and lesser additions of Trebbiano or the local Minella Bianca.

What both these growing areas share are mineral-rich soils derived from petrified lava that has been broken down over the centuries by lichens, grasses, wild fennel plants and broom. But while Salina's volcanic activity has long been extinct, Mount Etna is notorious for its protracted bursts of fire, compounded in recent years by earthquakes that have also incurred damage.

The wine estates on Salina are Lilliputian, with narrow, vine-clad terraces overlooking the azure sea and a profusion of scented caper plants adding to the local economy. The smallest of the quality producers is probably Francesco Fenech, whose organic Malvasia is obtained from just three hectares of vineyard; the Barone di Villagrande winery from Mount Etna has seven hectares

∩ *View over the small, terraced vineyard belonging to the Barone di Villagrande winery on the island of Salina.*

Pietramarina

Benanti

Etna Bianco Superiore DOC – white wine left to mature on its yeasts for at least 12 months in steel vats, followed by ageing for 5 months in the bottle

Carricante 100%

Its fruity elegance will persist and evolve for several years

Rich, intense and fruity on the nose, with hints of orange blossom and ripe apples; dry and harmonious in the mouth, with pleasant acidity, aromatic persistence and a touch of anise and almond on the finish

All fish and seafood dishes

Etna Rosso

Tenuta Scilio

Etna Rosso DOC – red wine fermented in steel vats, no barrel ageing

Nerello Mascalese 80%, Nerello Cappuccio 20%

5-6 years at least

Along with the fruit, a deceptive hint of wood on the nose; fruity, yet restrained and elegant in the mouth, with quite distinctive tannins

Mushroom soups, meats, pulses

of Malvasia on Salina and produces what is probably the island's finest raisin wine; the Tasca d'Almerita family have recently invested in 20 hectares, some of which will need replanting; and the Hauner winery, the largest on the island, adds to its own yields by purchasing grapes from other growers, yet still only produces an annual total of 40,000 bottles, including four different table wines. In neither of these growing areas have the international grape varieties, cultivated to such acclaim elsewhere on the island, found great favour. While this has an obvious logistical explanation in the case of Salina, their paucity on Etna probably has more to do with the area's established identity and tradition. The wineries tend to be relatively small and run by local patrician families: the Scammacca del Murgo family cultivates 25 hectares of vineyard on their estate at Santa Venerina; the Nicolosis at Villagrande just 18. And nor are the relative newcomers much larger. The beautifully positioned 20-hectare Tenuta Scilio winery at Valle Galfina near Giarre comprises 17 hectares of vineyard. Even the Benanti winery, whose search for typical Etnean features has led it to acquire vineyards in all of the viticultural microzones of Etna, does not go beyond 15 hectares.

What all these winemakers have in common is an impelling emotional and practical attachment to tradition, to their own oenological history. Though this does not entirely exclude a little Cabernet Sauvignon here and a touch of Chardonnay there, it does mean that producers are first and foremost set on getting their own local grape varieties to express themselves in unmistakable terms. Under the sensitive and wise direction of oenologist Salvo Foti, unquestionably the island's foremost expert on Etnean vines and rural traditions, the Benanti winery has not only contributed to the growing international renown of the Etna DOCs, but has also made a mission out of creating single variety wines from the local grape varieties. *I Monovitigni*, as the resultant collection of wines is called, offers a fascinating and slightly austere initiation into an almost magical universe.

↻ *The Scilio winery at Valle Galfina near Linguaglossa on Mount Etna.*

↻ *The San Michele estate at the Murgo winery near S. Venerina on Mount Etna.*

A Curiosity

Since no picture is complete without the exception that confirms the rule, mention must also be made of the Gurrida estate located above the town of Randazzo, within the Park of Mount Etna. The property comprises 170 hectares, covering a plateau and the surrounding slopes at an altitude of 850 metres and more. Here at the end of every winter, when the ice melts on the higher reaches of the mountain, the neighbouring river Flascio breaks its banks and inundates an extensive stretch of land lying within the plateau. This includes 36 hectares of densely planted vineyard, which is thus submerged under water from late October to mid March.

Viticulturalists who have never actually seen the gnarled, unpruned vines protruding from the mirror of water that reflects the blues and whites of a winter sky refuse to believe that survival is possible in such conditions. But this is no ordinary vineyard. It was planted during the early 1800s with Grenache, the French grape variety, at the behest of Lord Nelson, whose naval activities in the Mediterranean so pleased the Bourbon rulers of Naples and Sicily that they granted him the duchy of Bronte here on Etna. Moreover, since phylloxera, the destructive root-feeding aphid, cannot proliferate in water, the Gurrida vineyard was not wiped out during the pandemic of the late 19th and early 20th centuries. Almost uniquely, no grafting onto pest-resistant rootstocks has thus been necessary. When, after World War II, the vine training system was changed to replace the traditional "alberello" ("small tree") with the more manageable trellis, where necessary plants were replaced by propagation. At intervals along the rows, the original "mother" vines are still to be seen.

When in the late 1960s Lord Nelson's substantial property on Mount Etna was divided up and sold, the Cesarò family of nearby Giarre purchased the Gurrida estate. Lawyer turned agriculturalist Angelo Cesarò set to work on the abandoned vineyard in 1990, and from it he now produces a curiously intense, velvety red IGT that he has called *Victory*, in memory of Nelson's flagship at the battle of Trafalgar.

As a footnote to this curious story, suffice it to add that Cesarò has recently planted 4.5 hectares of Merlot on his property at 850 metres above sea level, and a further 1.5 hectares at 900 metres. To elude the late frosts that are not uncommon at such altitudes, the pruners are instructed to preserve one extra, tardy bud, so that any loss due to frozen shoots can be partly recovered when the days grow reliably mild.

Victory	
Gurrida	
IGT – red wine with no barrel ageing	
Grenache 100%	
5 years	
Intense and composite on the nose; rounded and substantial in the mouth, with good fruit, a touch of mineral and great persistence	
Seasoned cheeses, salami, cold cuts, game, red meats	

A Glance at the Future

Wines, like other consumer goods, are subject to fashions. And where fashions are based on substance, traditions can be established. At present, the grape variety that everyone is talking

➲ *The submerged vineyard at the Gurrida estate near Randazzo on Mount Etna, photographed in late March, when the waters are gradually withdrawing.*

about is Nero d'Avola. In relation to where it is grown, its deep, ruby red colour and aromas of ripe berries can be accompanied by a hint of tobacco, chocolate or even liquorice. Though it is widespread throughout Sicily's viticultural zones, excluding Etna, it actually only accounts for 11% of the island's overall production of wine grapes. As the name suggests, it was originally selected, several centuries ago, at Avola, a municipality in the province of Siracusa, in southeast Sicily. From here it spread slightly west and further south to the grape growing areas around Noto and Pachino, which are all now considered its true homeland and thus the terroir that can bring out its most authentic features.

In recent years both Pachino and the Noto area have attracted considerable investment on the part of farsighted winemakers. These include the Sicilians Planeta, Benanti and Vito Catania, owner of the Gulfi winery, as well as the Tuscans Filippo Mazzei (Fonterutoli) and Antonio Moretti (Tenuta Sette Ponti), and the Venetian industrialist, Paolo Marzotto.

Planeta has just finished building a new winery on its property near Noto. "It's actually quite exciting to be part of a new venture and knowing that a handful of top quality producers are also acting on the same perception of the area's potential", says Alessio Planeta. "Since this is the fatherland of Nero d'Avola, the local Eloro DOC is bound to take off in coming years. The appellation is based on Nero d'Avola, plus two other reds, Frappato di Vittoria and Pignatello. Although there are already producers of Eloro DOC, the appellation has a very hazy identity for consumers, since the name conjures up neither place nor grape variety".

After several vintages of experimentation, Planeta is also ready to bottle another local appellation: the Moscato di Noto, a dessert wine made with a variety of Muscat grape related to the Moscato d'Asti grown in Piedmont. Though this DOC was actually established back in 1974, it has long been bereft of quality producers. "This means that we have had to work without referring to a model, to something that already exists. What we bottled in

⌒ *Nino Pupillo, who has saved the luscious, sweet Moscato di Siracusa from oblivion.*

⌒ *Planeta's Buonivini vineyard near Noto.*

2003 is thus a tradition that we have reinvented", explains Alessio. And since what the Planetas do today, others feel inspired to try tomorrow, the chances are that within the space of a decade the Moscato di Noto DOC will have other subscribers.

The Planetas are convinced that certain well-defined appellations will help consumers orientate themselves in the complex and heady universe of Sicilian wine. It is also probable that they predict a return of interest in what are commonly, and reductively, called dessert wines.

This being so – and it seems more than plausible – another appellation that is bound to come to the fore in future years is the Moscato di Siracusa DOC, made with the same grape variety, but in a lower-lying area closer to the coast. The wine owes its being to the Greek colonisation of the south east of Sicily between the 8th and the 7th century BC, when King Pollium introduced from his native Thrace vines renowned for their sweet smelling mature grapes. Though in early modern times the Moscato di Siracusa was still widely appreciated, winning a gold medal for quality at the Paris Exhibition of 1900, by the late 20th century it had sunk into relative oblivion.

Happily, Nino Pupillo has breathed new life into a time-honoured tradition. Starting in 1991 with a single hectare of experimental vineyard, he now cultivates 12 hectares of Moscato and has been producing delightfully elegant sweet wines since his first vintage in 1997. He is currently restoring the majestically fortified family property, the Feudo della Targia, which should shortly become the headquarters for his entire winery. This, like all quality winegrowing, is an act of faith in a rewarding future.

So gradually the wine map of Sicily is getting clearer in its contours, with significant areas growing in colour and consistency. In future years, the DOCs that are too insubstantial to survive beyond their registration on paper could perhaps be embraced in a new and wider category of Sicilian table wines, thereby losing the distinction of the appellation but gaining in marketable appeal.

⋂ *Careful harvesting at the Pupillo winery near Siracusa.*

➲ *Muscat grapes nearly ready for harvesting, near Noto.*

Itineraries

It would take many months to visit all the wineries that are currently making Sicily one of the world's most exciting winemaking regions. Though the island certainly merits protracted attention, for most people the available time and resources fall within narrower confines. Bearing this in mind, the second section of the book takes a look at six of the island's foremost winegrowing areas, describing not only some of the winemakers themselves, but also the grape varieties, the landscape and the climate, and how they all relate to what ends up in the bottle.

While these are not detailed itineraries of the turn-right-here, turn-left-there variety, they will help those travelling through Sicily understand the wine they are drinking and what else to look out for. Hopefully the section will also help bibulous armchair travellers find their way round certain shelves at their local wine store.

Yet despite the best intentions, a book such as this inevitably has its shortcomings. While all the wineries mentioned in these itineraries are good or even excellent producers, there are many more quality winemakers who do not feature. It is practically impossible to be exhaustive, especially in a situation that is evolving so fast. But the book will have achieved an acceptable goal if it provides the reader with a few useful points of reference in the pursuit of pleasure.

Another limitation of itineraries based on the classic winegrowing areas lies in the fact that wineries located off the beaten viticultural track are likely to be left out. This is outstandingly the case of the Budonetto winery established in 1998 by Francesco Maurigi at Piazza Armerina, not far from the famous Villa del Casale. Viticulture was non-existent in this inland location until Maurigi defied local custom and planted Cabernet Sauvignon, Syrah, Merlot, Pinot Noir, Petit Verdot, Chardonnay and Sauvignon Blanc. With Giovanni Rizzo as his consultant oenologist, in less than a decade he has created wines of great elegance and promise. Though far removed from traditional winegrowing in Sicily, they may be opening up the way for future developments. In other words, a new itinerary may now be in the making.

The Baglio

From the 17th to the 19th centuries, western Sicily in particular was divided into large landed estates run by agents for absentee landlords living in Palermo. Feudal in structure and often far removed from towns of any importance, these properties revolved around a distinctive architectural complex known as a baglio. The word itself derives from the Latin vallum, meaning 'bastion', or from the Arabic bahal, meaning 'courtyard' or 'enclosure'.

Baglio San Vincenzo, near Menfi in the Province of Agrigento.

Based on a quadrangular plan, the baglio was often fortified and consisted of a massive outer wall with an imposing arched entrance leading through to the courtyard within. Embellished with windows and balconies, the residence designed for the landowner's infrequent visits rose proudly above the surrounding buildings. On the ground floor there were storerooms for farm produce, stables and the labourers' dwellings. Outside the main enclosure was a chapel used both by the landowner and by those who worked for him. Though many a crumbling and abandoned baglio is to be seen in the countryside of western Sicily, a number of them have been restored to their original splendour by wineries such as Baglio Hopps and Baglio Oneto. Such emblematic architecture clearly brings with it added value in terms of image. Further examples of an urban version of the same architectural scheme are to be found within Marsala itself, especially down on the waterfront. The grandest is the headquarters of the historic Florio winery, one of the earliest commercial producers of Marsala.

Heading out from Palermo

From DOCs to IGTs

Within striking distance of Palermo there are a number of highly significant wineries. There are also three DOCs, each worthy of note, but for different reasons. Yet the renown of the wineries seldom coincides, even partially, with the importance of the appellations. In other words, the winemakers who look to Palermo as their point of urban reference have mostly developed a distinctive profile of their own that precedes or transcends the collective identity of a DOC.

Established in 1972, the white Alcamo DOC straddles the provinces of Palermo and Trapani, and is one of Sicily's oldest appellations. It is also the second most productive, Marsala taking absolute pride of place. Yet output is actually declining, now accounting for less than 10% of the island's total DOC production, down from the 22% of the early 1990s. Moreover, it is not an appellation that conjures up images of fine wine, though there are some perfectly acceptable examples of Alcamo DOC.

The case is emblematic, in that it helps explain the individualism of the quality wineries and the existence of the other two appellations.

The older of the two is Contea di Sclafani DOC, which was founded in 1996 and comprises a wide range of whites, reds and a rosé, both as blends and as varietals of indigenous and international grape varieties. To some extent the appellation is a projection of the Tasca d'Almerita winery, though not exclusively so. However, the location of this sovereign Sicilian wine estate 90 kilometres southeast of Palermo probably explains why the DOC belongs not only to the province of Palermo, but also to slices of the bordering provinces of Caltanissetta and Agrigento.

Monreale DOC, on the other hand, occupies a relatively circumscribed area of gently rolling countryside between Palermo and Alcamo. Likewise heterogeneous, it was established in 2000 with support from wineries that immediately invested it with a quality image. The undeclared aim must surely have been to lend credence to the concept of appellations as such, but without having to marry into the unprepossessing family of Alcamo DOC.

The Great and the Good

Decades before anyone thought of proclaiming Sicily to be the new hot spot for quality wines there were three wineries on the island that had already reached out to oenophiles well beyond the national borders. They are the historic and indeed aristocratic forerunners of what became a trend. Without their proactive planting and planning, much of what has since come in their wake would have failed to materialize.

The first of these is Tasca d'Almerita, which is still at the forefront of Sicilian winemaking at its best. Currently run by Count Lucio Tasca d'Almerita and his sons Giuseppe and Alberto, together with general manager Gaetano Zangara (ex Corvo), the Regaleali estate has been in the hands of the Tasca family since 1830. Located between Vallelunga in the province of Caltanissetta and Valledolmo in the province of Palermo, the property comprises olive groves and 360 hectares of vineyard stretching out across a truly glorious, rolling landscape 400 to 750 metres above sea level.

⋂ *View of the vineyards at Regaleali, the Tasca d'Almerita estate at Vallelungo south east of Palermo.*

⮑ *Stainless steel vats at the Regaleali winery.*

Principe di Corleone Bianco

Pollara

Alcamo Bianco DOC – white wine whose components are vinified separately, then blended

Catarratto 80%, Damaschino 20%

2 years

Full-bodied fruity aromas; good balance in the mouth, with hints of vanilla and exotic fruits, and quite a long finish

Seafood, shellfish, soft cheeses

Sixteen grape varieties, with a substantial focus on Nero d'Avola and Inzolia, are grown commercially for the production of an admirable range of 5 reds, 5 whites, a rosé, a Novello and a sparkling wine. The fact that five of these belong to the Contea di Sclafani DOC largely accounts for that appellation's importance. Moreover, ten hectares are devoted to experimental vine growing involving 80 varieties, some of them of far-flung origin. The idea is to try them out in relation to the particular terroir. This is a winery of excellence with a vocation for research that dates back three generations.

The first to pursue quality was Lucio's father, Count Giuseppe Tasca, who introduced trellised spalliera-trained vines in the late 1960s. The estate was also innovative in applying short pruning techniques to obtain lower yields with richer aromas. Furthermore, it preceded others in reappraising local grape varieties and completing Nero d'Avola varietals with a little barrique-ageing. Alongside this, early experiments with Chardonnay and Cabernet Sauvignon opened up new vistas for Sicilian viticulture.

The Tasca d'Almerita's flagship wine is the *Rosso del Conte Contea di Sclafani DOC*, a Nero d'Avola blended with a very small percentage of Perricone (less than 10% for the 2000 vintage). This is a beautifully balanced, barrel-aged ruby red wine with a slightly spicy nose and palate.

Another wine estate of aristocratic origins is Duca di Salaparuta, founded in 1824 by Giuseppe Alliata, Prince of Villafranca and Duke of Salaparuta. A man of progressive ideas and considerable connoisseurship of wine, the duke decided to make his own wine from the Inzolia grapes grown on his property in the Corvo district of Casteldaccia, due east and slightly south of Palermo. The aim was to produce a wine that could be served to his eminent guests at Villa Valguarnera, his palatial residence.

Corvo was actually registered as a brand in 1874, and the wine itself found widespread admirers, not least among the royal courts of Europe. By the early 1900s, to meet demand the winery was buying grapes from growers throughout the island. This policy, and the

implications it had for employment, meant that when in 1961 the Salaparuta descendants found themselves in financial difficulties following heavy investments it was the Sicilian regional government that took over the property.

During the following decades Corvo enjoyed marked expansion in Europe, and by the 1990s was able to modernise and refurbish the cellars. Then, in 2001, the whole winery was re-privatised, ending up in the hands of the drinks conglomerate Ilva of Saronno, that had already taken over the historic Cantine Florio of Marsala. In so doing it lost both its acclaimed winemaker, Franco Giacosa, who accepted an offer from Zonin, and Gaetano Zangara, the chief executive who was snapped up by Regaleali.

The technical direction of this vast enterprise with its 10 million bottle annual output had been entrusted to Carlo Casavecchia, the Piedmont-trained winemaker with a track record that comprises Florio and Cinzano. It is early days to judge this new stage in the winery's history. Nevertheless, the *Duca Enrico Nero d'Avola* varietal

continues to exercise a certain charm, at least on the contributors to a number of influential wine guides.

The third of Palermo's time-honoured wineries is Rapitalà, a toponym that derives from the Arabic *Rabidh-Allah*, meaning "the river of Allah". Located at an altitude of 300 to 600 metres, this auspiciously named estate embraces gentle slopes in the vicinity of Camporeale, a little southwest of Palermo. It belonged to the Guarrasi family of Palermo, whose daughter Gigi in 1968 married the Frenchman Comte Hugues Bernard de la Gatinais.

That same year an earthquake destroyed much of the Belice valley, extending its calamitous effects to the winery on the Rapitalà property. Thereafter the newly wed couple set about rebuilding and modernising the facilities, introducing new equipment and planting grape varieties such as Chardonnay and Pinot Nero in the clay-rich, sandy soils that had hitherto seen only Catarratto and Nero d'Avola. In more recent years the energies and image of the winery seemed to be flagging slightly. However, a substantial injection of financial

⊃ The Ceuso vineyards planted in the clayey, calcareous soils of the Alcamo hillsides, an area traditionally devoted to white wines. Significantly, Ceuso has opted for reds.

⊃ View overlooking the Alcamo depot area where Baglio Ceuso is located.

⊃ The barrique cellar at the Spadafora estate, south west of Palermo.

and management input on the part of GIV (Gruppi Italiano Vini), the largest wine company in Italy, is now gradually helping the estate fine tune its future profile.

The 175-hectare Rapitalà estate currently comprises 128 hectares of vineyard planted with Syrah, Pinot Nero Cabernet Sauvignon and Chardonnay, as well as the traditional Nero d'Avola and Catarratto. As a tribute to the winery's location in the vicinity of Alcamo, its major seller, the *I Templi* range, comprises a perfectly acceptable Catarratto varietal that belongs to the Alcamo DOC and a Nero d'Avola made for early drinking.

The other wines range from the inexpensive *Piano Maltese* white (70/30% blend of Catarratto and Chardonnay), red (Nero d'Avola) and rosé (Nerello Mascalese and Perricone) to the far more imposing deep, chocolaty *Solinero* Syrah varietal, the thoroughly pleasant *Hugonis* barrique-aged 60/40% Cabernet Sauvignon/Nero d'Avola blend, or the fresh and balanced *Casalj* marriage of Catarratto and Chardonnay. For the consumer, the sensation is that Rapitalà can be a little uneven in its core products, which are the ones most readily found in wine stores further afield. Hopefully the new direction of the winery will iron out such inconsistencies and reconfirm the prestige of a label that has played a role for Sicily: though Tasca d'Almerita may have been the island's ambassador, Rapitalà was still a worthy consul.

The Young Lions

There are several remarkable wineries south east of Palermo, a little more than a stone's throw from Alcamo. Although one of them (Cusumano) does actually include an Alcamo DOC in its output, the others seem disinclined to have anything to do with the appellation. Indeed, for all of them the main quality focus is on red wines: a sort of declaration of independence; a countertrend that could prove more rewarding than the mainstream products for which the area has gained a name.

Closest to Palermo and possibly to the local winemaking tradition is the Cusumano winery at Paceco. Grapes have been grown on the property

Leone d'Almerita		
🏠	Tasca d'Almerita	
🍾	White wine with no barrel ageing	
🍇	Catarratto 65%, Chardonnay 30% Sauvignon 5%	
🕐	3–5 years	
🍷	Apply and peachy aromas on the nose, with a hint of banana and pineapple: fresh and aromatic in the mouth, with plenty of personality	
🍴	Pasta dishes, fowl, rabbit, seafood	

Nuhar		
🏠	Rapitalà	
🍾	IGT - red wine, partially aged for one year in barriques	
🍇	Nero d'Avola 70%, Pinot Nero 30%	
🕐	3 years	
🍷	Spicey and quite intense in the mouth; elegant without being heavy	
🍴	Pasta dishes with meat sauce, feathered game, cheese	

Gran Cru Chardonnay		
🏠	Rapitalà	
🍾	IGT – white wine, two thirds of which is aged on the yeasts for 12 months in barriques before being reunited with the other third and aged in the bottle prior to release	
🍇	Chardonnay 100%	
🕐	2–3 years	
🍷	Aromatic, but clean on the palate and with no prevarication from the wood. Rounded and substantial in the mouth, with a pleasantly fresh, long finish	
🍴	Fowl, rabbit, fish, seasoned cheese	

for over forty years, but only became acclaimed wines when Francesco Cusumano handed over the management to his handsome scions, Alberto and Diego. With their business acumen and feeling for what the market will appreciate, they have produced a wide range of wines (five whites and six reds) that all speak for themselves with a certain authority and elegance. An eloquent case in point is the *Noà IGT*, an attractive, balanced 40/30/30% blend of Nero d'Avola, Merlot and Cabernet Sauvignon. The 140-hectare estate comprises 70 hectares of vineyard, including a new property up near Piana degli Albanesi. While the white grapes are harvested in the neighbouring areas of Alcamo, Monreale, Grisì and Salemi, the reds come from further afield, including Mazara del Vallo on the west coast, Contessa Entellina due south, and Pachino at the south-eastern tip of the island. It is arguably this ability to source and select grapes from different terroirs that gives the Cusumano wines their consistently distinctive identities.

Down in the old terminal area of Alcamo, where much of the wine was once stored prior to shipping, there is a fine old agricultural complex enclosed behind high walls called Baglio Ceuso. Built in 1860, when large quantities of Marsala left this corner of the province of Trapani for markets abroad, it has just been restored to accommodate the cellars and offices of the Ceuso winery.

This brilliant example of Sicily's wine renaissance owes its being to an excellent team: the three Melia brothers, Antonino, who looks after the vineyards, Giuseppe and Vincenzo, who combine the expertise of oenology and agronomy. Vincenzo juggles the demands of their 40-hectare estate with his job as the most senior agronomist at the *Istituto Regionale della Vite e del Vino*. He has thus overseen most of the planting of experimental vineyards across Sicily over the past 20 years, using the knowledge obtained in this research in his role as advisor to many of the island's foremost wineries. Indeed, his outstanding skills are now sought by wineries in mainland Italy contemplating important new planting projects, which is a telling reversal of the Sicily-bound expertise characteristic of earlier years. The Melia brothers began planting their new vineyards in 1990,

Ceuso Custera	
Ceuso	
IGT – red wine fermented in steel, aged for 12 months in 225 litre French casks, in old concrete vats for 4 months and in the bottle for 18 months	
Nero d'Avola 50%, Cabernet Sauvignon 30%, Merlot 20%	
8–10 years	
Full-bodied, with fine tannins and a long, complete finish	
Roasted meats, stews, game, mushrooms and seasoned cheese	

Schietto - Syrah	
Spadafora	
IGT – red wine aged for 12 months in barriques and 6 months in the bottle	
Syrah 100%	
10 years	
Rich aromas of berries; full in the mouth, with excellent balance and elegant tannins	
White meats, roasted meats, game	

The rolling vinescape of Contrada Virzì, near Camporeale, where the Principi di Spadafora estate is located.

forsaking their father's white grape varieties for reds, largely Nero d'Avola, plus a little Cabernet Franc and Merlot. "Our idea was to heed what the market wants", Vincenzo explains. "Though this is thought of as being an area for white wines, we felt that our calcareous, clayey soils, our dry summers, breezy springs and adequate winter rainfall were ideal for certain reds. So instead of insisting on Catarratto, we decided to make an important red wine with distinctly Mediterranean features".

The outcome was *Ceuso Custera*, a 50/30/20% blend of the above varieties that first appeared in 1995 and immediately impressed all those who tasted it. Since then a growing number of Ceuso aficionados have also welcomed *Ceuso Fastaia*, a Nero d'Avola with a touch (15%) of Cabernet Franc and Merlot that is elegant, complex and a far cry from the rather obvious, show-off reds that western Sicily can also produce.

Over the years Vincenzo Melia has come into close contact with the doyen of Italian oenologists, Giacomo Tachis, whose name is linked to some of the country's most prestigious wines. Happily for Sicily, Tachis has become the island's foremost adviser and supporter in its new viticultural developments, interfacing regularly with the *Istituto Regionale della Vite e del Vino* and with many individual wineries.

As the second chapter of the first part of this book outlined briefly, one of Tachis's more recent tenets is that steel is to be eschewed for protracted maturation because it can build up electromagnetic charges that affect the evolution of the wine. He also believes that wines should not be filtered, since this removes the larger particles, which are the proteins, thus impeding the wine's further development. At Baglio Ceuso, alongside the steel still used for fermentation, the old concrete vats of the 1950s and 1960s have been restored and returned to use. The winery's most recent product is *Ceuso Scurati*, again a wine that represents a countertrend. It is a Nero d'Avola that is neither filtered nor aged in wood. Made for drinking young, it has plenty of fresh fruit that mingles with hints of chocolate and liquorice. Moreover, for such a handsome product it sells at a very reasonable price.

↷ Vineyards at the Baglio di Pianetto winery, on a highland near S. Cristina Gela, just south of Palermo.

↶ Vincenzo Melia, the most senior agronomist at the Istituto Regionale della Vite e del Vino and a driving force at the Melia brothers' Ceuso winery near Alcamo.

Scurati	
🏠	Ceuso
🍷	IGT – red wine with no barrel ageing
🍇	Nero d'Avola 100%
⏱	2 years
🍷	Plenty of fresh fruit on the nose and in the mouth, with hints of chocolate and liquorice
🍴	Pasta dishes, fowl, rabbit

Just the other side of Alcamo, heading south towards the little town of Camporeale, there is a wine estate that gained essential initial impetus from its close collaboration with the Regional Institute for Vines and Viticulture. The Azienda Agricola dei Principi di Spadafora is a 180-hectare property that stretches languidly across airy, undulating farmland at 220 to 450 metres above sea level. Traditionally it has been used for raising sheep as well as growing olives, prickly pears and grapes.

The original vineyards were planted in 1970, and since the estate lies within the Alcamo DOC, it was white varieties that prevailed: Catarratto and Inzolia, trained in the traditional *alberello alcamese* and planted at a density of 2000 plants per hectare.

Then, in the early 1990s, the Spadafora family planted trellis-trained experimental vineyards under the auspices of the *Istituto Regionale della Vite e del Vino*, lending their own cellars for the micro-vinification that now takes place in the Institute's own premises in Marsala. This in time led to the selection of Syrah, Cabernet Sauvignon and Merlot as being particularly well suited to the friable soils with their clayey nutrients that are typical of the area.

For over a decade now Francesco Spadafora has headed the winery with a light touch and considerable independence of spirit. Having left Palermo in favour of a landscape that evidently speaks to him in more eloquent terms, he has made simple, colourful accommodations out of the farm buildings, living in one of them himself and offering the others to his guests. Just behind his dwelling are the cellars, an outer wall of which is decorated with a bright, spray-painted mural. It is the work of a Palermo street-artist whose self-expression had hitherto been confined to urban sprawl and railway sidings. Initially incredulous of Francesco's offer of a paid a job, he has created a luminous symbol for the winery.

Francesco Spadafora's somewhat unconventional approach to things has led him, by his own confession, "to make endless mistakes" (not the expression he used) to do with planting and pruning. He must have learnt from these experiences, however, since both his reds and his

⋒ *Gentle, vine-clad hillsides at the Spadafora estate at Contrada Virzì, south west of Palermo.*

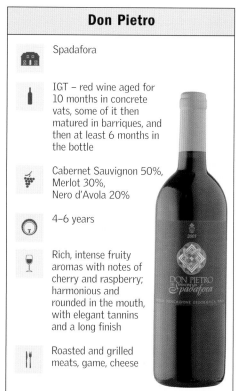

Don Pietro

Spadafora

IGT – red wine aged for 10 months in concrete vats, some of it then matured in barriques, and then at least 6 months in the bottle

Cabernet Sauvignon 50%, Merlot 30%, Nero d'Avola 20%

4–6 years

Rich, intense fruity aromas with notes of cherry and raspberry; harmonious and rounded in the mouth, with elegant tannins and a long finish

Roasted and grilled meats, game, cheese

whites are highly individual, and yet rounded and balanced as well. Outstanding among them is the *Schietto Rosso IGT*, a rich, plummy Syrah with hints of chocolate and tobacco. It comes as no surprise to discover that the available Alcamo DOC has been spurned in favour of the newly founded Monreale DOC. In fact the *Alhambra Monreale Bianco DOC*, made from the grapes grown in those sparsely planted but by now elderly vineyards, is Spadafora's one concession to appellations. Not far from here is another winery that is likely to attract admirers in coming years. Azienda Agricola Alessandro di Camporeale is a 45-hectare property with 35 hectares of vineyard planted at an altitude of 480 metres on sunny hillsides overlooking the Belice Valley, between the municipalities of Camporeale and Monreale. Involved in viticulture for generations, the Alessandro family today counts on its youngest scions, the three brothers Antonino, Rosolino and Natale, to make the quality leap. In this they are led by Antonino, a consultant agronomist specialized in viticulture whose wife, Lia Arcuri, a chemist by profession, also cultivates a passion for wine.

The existing Alessandro vineyards have been reconverted, and new ones planted with Syrah, Merlot, Cabernet Sauvignon, Cabernet Franc and Chardonnay as well as Nero d'Avola. Moreover, new cellars have just been built and fitted with state-of-the-art equipment. Under guidance from Sicilian oenologist Vincenzo Bambina (a name that comes up time and again among the outstanding smaller wineries of Sicily), the first vintage was the 2000 *Kaid Syrah IGT*. This is a beautifully balanced barrique-aged wine full of fruit that portends well for the future, when it should be joined by a Nero d'Avola.

A Few Older Lions, With Plenty of Growl

Though the district covered in these pages is certainly pulsating with youthful energy, there are also various forward-looking wineries that are firmly in the hands of a slightly older generation endowed with the flexibility and foresight to move with the times. One such case in point is the Principe di Corleone estate run by the Pollara family.

↻ ◑ *Francesco Spadafora (above) got a Palermo graffiti artist to paint this wall, which has become a luminous symbol of the whole winery.*

Pippo, Vincenzo and Lea Pollara founded the new family winery in 1979, in the heart of what has since become the Monreale DOC. Their output is the fruit of ongoing research and a keen nose for subtle changes in the market. They currently produce a considerable range of wines, including the award-winning *Principe di Corleone Nero d'Avola* and an acclaimed *Alcamo Bianco DOC*. While this latter is a classic 80/20% Catarratto/Damaschino blend, the estate largely focuses on single-variety wines: not only the local Nero d'Avola and Inzolia, but also a Pinot Bianco, a Sauvignon Blanc, a Chardonnay, a Cabernet Sauvignon and a Merlot.

Another estate with a well-seasoned leader at the helm is Baglio di Pianetto, located at an altitude of 600 to 700 metres in the hills due south of Palermo, at Santa Cristina Gela. It is the brainchild and progeny elect of Count Paolo Marzotto, a Venetian businessman with interests in insurance and textiles as well as wine. With an energy that belies his 70-plus years, Marzotto has succumbed to his love of Sicily, planting vineyards at Pachino in the south-eastern tip of the island, and up in the hills behind Palermo, where his splendid new winery is just nearing completion.

While the Pachino vineyards focus on Nero d'Avola, the 80 hectares at Santa Cristina Gela are largely devoted to indigenous whites such as Inzolia, and Merlot and Petit Verdot for the reds. The *Ramione IGT* is a blend of Nero d'Avola (50%), Merlot (40%) and Petit Verdot (10%) that draws on the characteristics of both wine-producing areas. Deep ruby in colour, to the nose it offers berries, tobacco and spices, while in the mouth it is rich and fruity, with a hint of nutmeg on the finish.

It is probable, however, that the flagship Ramione along with the other three wines currently produced by this estate will take a few years to settle down and establish their true identities. This is partly because newly planted or reconverted vineyards obviously take time to come into their own; but also because the cellars themselves were not entirely ready for production when the wines were first launched, which meant that certain stages of the vinification had to take place elsewhere.

Principe di Corleone – Il Rosso

- Pollara
- IGT Riserva – red wine aged for 18 months in 5000 litre casks and 3–4 months in barriques
- Nero d'Avola 100%
- 5–6 years
- Fragrant and complex to the nose; warm, dry, full-bodied yet elegant in the mouth
- Game, roasted and grilled meats; firm cheeses

Ramione

- Baglio di Pianetto
- IGT – red wine aged for 10 months in concrete vats, some of it then matured in barriques, and then at least 6 months in the bottle
- Cabernet Sauvignon 50%, Merlot 30%, Nero d'Avola 20%
- 4–6 years
- Rich, intense fruity aromas with notes of cherry and raspberry; harmonious and rounded in the mouth, with elegant tannins and a long finish
- Roasted and grilled meats, game, cheese

☊ *Abundant growth on healthy vines at the Abbazia Santa Anastasia winery at Castelbuono, overlooking the Cefalù coastline due east of Palermo.*

To conclude this itinerary *in bellezza*, the focus swings due east, to Castelbuono, a town in the Madonie hills overlooking the coastal resort of Cefalù. Though this area is said to have produced wines of excellence in the late Middle Ages, when in 1980 builder Francesco Lena purchased the Abbazia Santa Anastasia, a derelict 12th century Benedictine monastery, there had been no significant viticulture in the area in living memory.

Lena's original intention was to develop this magnificent hillside by creating holiday homes for the discerning and moneyed few. Happily, as he paced around his magnificent 460-hectare estate, he underwent an almost Pauline conversion, accompanied by a vision of the wines that his terroir could produce.

Far from building chalets and clubhouses, he terraced the hillsides and set about planting new vineyards, under the guidance of Vincenzo Melia from the *Istituto Regionale della Vite e del Vino*. The main varieties are Cabernet Sauvignon, Merlot, Nero d'Avola and Nerello Mascelese for the reds, and Chardonnay, Inzolia and Grecanico for the whites. In due course cellars were built, and later enlarged and improved. With initial advice from Giacomo Tachis and further consultancy from Riccardo Cotarella, both of them blessed with oenological genius, the wines produced by Abbazia Santa Anastasia are simply excellent.

Meanwhile Francesco Lena has turned his developer's eye to other products, including olive oil and cheeses made from the milk of sheep grazing on the property. He has also restored the abbey, turning it into a luxury hotel with spa facilities, and begun to focus on an ample swathe of land destined to become a golf course. Though the odd holiday house may still find its way into the picture, the estate also comprises experimental vineyards and a winemaking research facility. As the impressive *Montenero* blend of Nero d'Avola, Merlot and Cabernet Franc goes to show, the quality of the wines is an established fact. Indeed, the *Litra* blend of Cabernet Sauvignon and Nero d'Avola has already achieved the status of a cult wine, thereby confirming the Abbey's original vocation.

🎧 *Vines surrounding the Abbazia Santa Anastasia. The complex now comprises a luxury hotel as well as the winery.*

Passomaggio

Abbazia Santa Anastasia

IGT – red wine aged for 9 months in barriques and 6 months in the bottle

Nero d'Avola 80%, Merlot 20%

4 years

Plenty of ripe fruit on the nose; fragrance, body and fine smooth tannins in the mouth

Pasta dishes with vegetable and meat sauces, hare, meat stews

The West Coast:
Trapani and Marsala

The Lie of the Land

Although the Province of Trapani extends to the east as far as the important winegrowing town of Alcamo, for the purpose of this itinerary it makes better sense to focus on the coastal area. The reason for this is the fact that the western seaports of Marsala and Trapani share more than a common vocation for winemaking. Separated by thirty kilometres of coastal road, both have important links with Antiquity, tracing their independent origins back to the 4th century BC and succumbing, as cities, to Roman domination in 241 BC. Moreover both, in the course of time, acquired strategic and mercantile importance as a maritime crossroads with Africa.

Indeed, from Africa came not only Arab peoples and culture, but also the strong, dry winds that have always been a seasonal trait of the two low-lying coastal towns. For around the western extremity of Sicily, annual rainfall rarely exceeds 500 mm, while mean annual temperatures easily reach 17.5 °C. Such a climate and location naturally favour the production of sea salt, once a mainstay of the local economy and still a feature of the landscape.

In winter, shallow mirrors of enclosed seawater reflect the changing

skies, the occasional windmill (once used for refining the salt) and long mounds of salt covered with pink and beige terracotta tiles to protect the yield from humidity and the wind. From February to March, seawater is pumped from a canal into salt-pans which decrease in depth to allow the salinity of the water to increase. By July the sun has evaporated the water from the last pan and the salt harvest can begin. Throughout the year the marshes provide birdlife with an interesting protected environment.

In the vicinity of the coast, the soils tend to be reddish in colour and not particularly fertile. This, along with the abundance of dry heat, allows winegrowers to obtain grapes with high sugar content, low overall acidity and a marked tendency to oxidation once crushed. This is actually of benefit for the production of Marsala, and can be controlled for making table wines.

Further inland from both towns is a hilly area with more clayey soils that are richer in humus. Average temperatures are a degree or two lower than those of the coast, annual rainfall is slightly higher, and the vineyards tend to produce higher yields, but with lower sugar content. Winemakers select their growing area in relation to the end product they have in mind.

Overlooking Trapani and the seascape beyond is a hill surmounted by the well-preserved medieval town of Erice. Isolated from the surrounding countryside by winter mists, the hillsides offer summer refuge from the intense heat of the lower lying areas for the many Trapanesi who have country properties among the vineyards in what has become a prime growing area.

There is also an attractive hilly area clad with olive groves and vineyards due east of Marsala. At first gentle in its elevation, the road leading there steepens and twists as it climbs up to Salemi, a town with two aspects: one that looks benignly towards the coast; and another that grimly faces the Belice valley, ravaged by an earthquake in 1968.

Though Trapani and Marsala both suffered during allied air raids in 1940 and 1943, they have seemingly recovered well: together with

Torre Dei Venti

Fazio Wines

IGT – red wine barrique aged for 8 months

Nero d'Avola 100%

8–10 years

Red berries, ripe cherries and spicy aromas on the nose. Full-bodied and velvety in the mouth, with a long finish

Medium seasoned cheeses, grilled or roasted meats, grilled fresh tuna

the surrounding province, they rate as the most densely vine-clad area in the whole of Italy. In fact the area comprises 66,000 hectares of vineyard, according to the 2001 census, and is also home to 50% of Sicily's cooperative wineries, a number of which produce wines of exceptional quality. Yet for all that they have in common, as towns Marsala and Trapani are as diverse as two independent-minded cousins.

Renewal in Trapani

With its population of 73,000, Trapani is actually smaller than Marsala, whose inhabitants number 80,000. Yet it is the provincial capital, boasting both a university (an offshoot of that of Palermo) and its own airport. It also has a pleasant historic centre, now a pedestrian precinct that shows off to considerable effect some fine baroque palazzi, recently restored to their former splendour.

For much of the late 20th century, Italians tended to equate Trapani with intense Mafia activity. Today this image is on the wane, making way instead for a certain aura of wellbeing that suggests the town is regaining some degree of the pride evident in its 17th and 18th century architecture.

Moreover, its table wines are deservedly making a name for themselves. Interesting results are being achieved with international grape varieties such as Chardonnay, Sauvignon and Viognier, as well as Cabernet Sauvignon, Syrah and Merlot. And the indigenous Grillo, Catarratto, Inzolia and Pignatello, once grown largely for producing Marsala, are now cultivated more selectively for the creation of fine IGTs (producers on the west coast appear to give little credence to the local DOCs). Happily there is also at least one restaurant in the area (Fontana in Via S. Giovanni Bosco) that has chosen to showcase what local wineries, and indeed Sicily as a whole, can produce.

Trapani's newfound dignity owes much to the Fazio family. For Girolamo Fazio has not only served the city well as its mayor, but together with his brother Vincenzo he has created a family winery

♪ *Salt pans and a mound of salt under the March sky of Marsala.*

that exports an image along with its excellent wines. Located at Fulgatore, on the south east side of Erice, Fazio Wines embodies an emblematic tale of the quest for quality.

The family estates had long produced grapes for wine, and in 1990 hired Giacomo Ansaldi, a Sicilian-born winemaker who had gained invaluable experience in Australia and New Zealand before returning to his homeland. Under Ansaldi's guidance, by 1998 Fazio Wines was ready to deliver its first estate-bottled products for critical appraisal. Within the space of five years recognition was flowing in from all quarters.

Fazio Wines, like other producers in this area, is eclectic in its output. While the local Pignatello and the indigenous Nero d'Avola constitute a central feature, some persuasive results are also obtained with Cabernet Sauvignon, Syrah, Petit Verdot and Merlot. Likewise the white varietals embrace the local Catarratto, Grillo and Inzolia as well as Chardonnay, Sauvignon Blanc, Müller Thurgau and Viognier, to say nothing of the recent additions of Fiano, a variety from the Campania region that seems to do well in western Sicily, and Gewürtztraminer. In all cases, clarification and filtering are disdained, in keeping with the Fazio philosophy whereby "each wine should speak for itself, and with a natural, distinctive voice".

However, the winery that has surpassed all others in showing what Sicily can achieve when its energies are well focused is the Cantina Sociale di Trapani. Founded in 1955 by 255 cooperative growers, it started off by producing and selling musts. The switch to fine bottled wines came in the mid 1990s, and involved persuading the growers that the future was in quality wines, not grape concentrates. Their numbers dropped to 145, but soon included a younger generation who understood the importance of producing premium grapes. A core of 7 growers produces around 60% of the winery's grapes, while the remaining 40% comes from "micro-growers" with 2 or 3 hectares of vineyard each. The growing area is between Trapani and Marsala, with vineyards yielding particular quality in the generous, stony soils at 280 metres altitude in the Erice valley.

Forti Terre di Sicilia-Cabernet Sauvignon

Cantina Sociale di Trapani

IGT – red wine, 70% of which aged for 10-12 months in new barriques

Cabernet Sauvignon 100%

7 years

Aromas of ripe fruit, plus a hint of vanilla; complex in the mouth, with plenty of spice and pleasant tannins

Roasted and grilled meats, tasty pasta dishes, mature cheese

PietraSacra

Fazio Wines

IGT – red wine each component of which is aged separately for 1 year in barriques, then blended and aged for a further year in the same barriques

Cabernet Sauvignon 60%, Nero d'Avola 30%, Merlot 10%

up to 15 years

Red berries with a hint of tabacco, cocoa, liquorice, black pepper. Full, smooth and persistent.

Red meats, game, roast leg of lamb

Inspiration and encouragement are always available from Roberto Adragna, the cooperative's chairman. Trained as a lawyer, Adragna is one of an increasingly rare breed of country gentlemen of great learning and foresight who like to describe themselves as farmers. Ever keen to empower the youngsters working at the winery by helping them realise their projects, he is happier sweeping the yard in contact with his protégés than sitting behind a desk in splendid isolation.

The Cantina Sociale di Trapani produces two categories of wine: the *Drepanum* line consisting of a red, a white, a rosé and a sparkling wine whose price/quality ratio make them ideal for trattoria consumption; and the admirable *Forti Terre di Sicilia* wines that have rightly met with widespread acclaim. Suffice it to mention the *1999 Cabernet Sauvignon* that won the coveted 3 Glasses Award (Italy's foremost wine accolade). Likewise remarkable are the *Chardonnay*, the *Nero d'Avola* and the blend of Inzolia (from the President's vineyards), Catarratto and Chardonnay. "Fortunately consumers are more confident and competent nowadays", Adragna explains. "A few years ago they only thought something was good if it was expensive. Major wineries get worried when they see us producing fine wines at the right price".

In its pursuit of excellence, the Cantina Sociale di Trapani has worked closely with a family of oenologists who are fast becoming a winemaking dynasty. Giovanni Centonze, the father, has now made way for his son Nicola, who was responsible for some exceptional winemaking while still in his twenties.

The remarkable Centonze family, including Nicola's sister Carla (Silvio Centonze, their cousin, is the oenologist at Rapitalà), also produce some interesting wines of their own under the Sicilia Vera label. Adragna has wisely facilitated this by letting them use the cooperative winery's infrastructure. "Youngsters will stay with you if you give them the chance to do something of their own. Nicola makes his wine here, and if he didn't we'd probably lose him".

The Centonzes use indigenous and international grape varieties to

⋒ *Roberto Adragna (right), his son Goffredo (centre) and Nicola Centonze, the brilliant young oenologist at the Cantina Sociale di Trapani.*
↻ *Winter pruning at the Donnafugata winery at Contessa Entellina, inland from Marsala towards the Belice valley.*

Forti Terre di Sicilia -Chardonnay

Cantina Sociale di Trapani

White wine fermented in steel and partially (40%) aged for 4 months barriques

Chardonnay 100%

1–2 years

Fresh and appley on the nose, with fruit and vanilla in fine balance; elegant and velvety in the mouth, again with a hint of golden apples

Vegetable pasta dishes, salmon, swordfish, white meats, salads, medium seasoned cheese

produce excellent varietals and well-balanced blends, creating, among other things, a pleasantly fresh white from the largely spurned Damaschino grape.

Nicola is clearly versatile in his skills, creating different styles of wine for different wineries. Nothing could be further removed from the products that come under his own family label than Serramarrocco, another of his creations. It is an extraordinarily intense, chocolaty blend of Cabernet Sauvignon and Merlot made at the Cantina Sociale for the neighbouring Serramarrocco estate.

The Adragna family, which includes Roberto's son Goffredo, also produce wines in their own right using premium grapes from their vineyards in the Erice valley. The Adragna label comprises a Chardonnay cru that is partly aged in wood, a Nero d'Avola that is not aged in wood, and a Cabernet Sauvignon blended with Merlot that is matured in barriques. To avoid any suggestion of a conflict of interest, these products are commercially handled by the Tuscany-based Classica wine merchants.

Just off the main road leading from Trapani to Marsala is Fondo Antico, a winery founded in 2000 and fitted with state-of-the-art equipment. Located at an altitude of 200 metres, southeast of Erice, the vineyards produce Nero d'Avola, Grillo and Inzolia, as well as Cabernet Sauvignon, Merlot, Syrah and Chardonnay. The first vintage, in 2002, comprised two wines, *Il Canto*, a 65/35% Nero d'Avola and Cabernet Sauvignon blend, and *Il Coro*, a rather buttery 50/50% Grillo and Chardonnay blend. It is, of course, early days to judge the winery's output. However, the fact that the oenologist is Vincenzo Bambina, a colleague of Nicola Centonze in a dynamic consultancy partnership, would seem to augur well for the future.

Marsala's Difficult Heritage

For all its rich archaeology and pleasant pedestrian district, industrious Marsala no longer appears to be quite the Harbour of God (*Mars-al-Allah*) its 9th century Saracen rulers believed it to be.

Bianco delle Magnolie	
🏠	Sicilia Vera Centonze
🍾	IGT – white wine
🍇	Inzolia 50%, Grillo 50%
🕐	1–2 years
🍷	Elegant, balanced, discreet, but with character
🍴	Seafood hors d'oeuvres, delicate fish dishes, white meats

Serramarrocco	
🏠	Tenuta di Serramarrocco
🍾	Red wine aged for 12 months in barriques, then 3–4 months in the bottle
🍇	Cabernet Sauvignon 85%, Merlot 15%
🕐	5–6 years
🍷	Complex nose full of fruit and some spice; full-bodied and distinctly chocolatey in the mouth
🍴	Red meats, game

↷ *Cool picks: the Donnafugata winery has introduced night-time harvesting at its Contessa Entellina estate.*

➲ *The imposing Pellegrino cellars where the Marsala is aged.*

Indeed, it actually comes across as a little unkempt, as if its inhabitants were too busy being the island's foremost wine producers to find the time for the urban-planning equivalent of combing their hair.

Marsala's fortunes, and thus its aspect, inevitably reflect those of its supreme ambassador, the fortified wine of the same name. This latter owes its being to an English merchant named John Woodhouse. In 1773, forced by a storm to seek refuge in the port of Marsala, Woodhouse sampled the local wine and decided to ship 60 large barrels of it home for the English market. To help it survive the long sea journey, he increased its alcohol content with grape spirit. By the time it reached its destination, the wine was somewhat reminiscent of Port and Madeira, which were already popular in England. In next to no time the Marsala wine was meeting with such acclaim that demand soon far outstripped supply.

Extensive new vineyards were thus planted, and another Englishman arrived to make his own fortune and consolidate that of the city. This was Benjamin Ingham, who founded a company in Marsala in 1812, introducing a number of technological improvements and exporting the wine further afield, to America and the Far East. His importance soon surpassed that of Woodhouse.

The first Italian concern to trade in what was still called "Madeira-style wine" was that of Vincenzo Florio, who in 1839 became sole proprietor of a company founded six years earlier. Though the family was advantageously involved in shipping, it took Florio twenty years to make his *baglio*, or winery, competitive. By 1856 he was winning awards at national and international events, taking over lesser companies and building storage space elsewhere in Sicily. Come 1880, his vast Marsala premises employed 300 workers and was able to produce 500,000 hectolitres of the wine per year. The Florio family diversified, getting involved in textiles, foundries, shipbuilding and fisheries.

Their fortunes took a down turn when phylloxera brought Sicilian viticulture to its knees in the early 1900s. In 1924 Florio & C. was sold

Il Canto

Fondo Antico

IGT – red wine aged for 15 months in French oak barriques and 6 months in the bottle

Nero d'Avola 65%, Cabernet Sauvignon 35%

5–6 years

Ripe fruit plus a touch of dried figs on the nose; soft and complex in the mouth, with plenty of ripe fruit followed by liquorice and chocolate

Fine red meats, mature cheeses

Marsala Superiore Riserva Oro Dolce

Buffa

Marsala DOC – fortified white wine aged for 4 years in large Slavonian oak casks followed by a further 2 years in small French oak casks

Grillo 100%

Evolves continuously with ageing

Complex aromas of dried figs, honey, almonds and vanilla; velvety sweet in the mouth with remarkable persistence

More of less seasoned cheeses, dry sweetmeats

to the Turin-based drinks group Cinzano; then in 1998 it was taken over by another vintner, ILLVA of Saronno, near Milan.

Today there are various companies producing Marsala, some of them historic, such as Florio and Pellegrino, some of them of more recent foundation. The Marsala DOC was established in 1964, and currently represents 60% of the Sicilian DOC wine output. Since the quantities of Marsala produced actually diminish substantially from one year to the next, this probably says more for the island's preference for IGTs than it does for the relative commercial strength of Marsala.

Indeed, in recent decades an aura of despondency has surrounded the dessert wine on which fortunes were once made. The reason for this may be partly explained by the cyclical fluctuations of taste. After decades of neglect, only now are sweet wines beginning to make a timid comeback. Yet it also has surely to do with some serious mismanagement of image. In an attempt to broaden their customer base, producers have resorted to some execrable concoctions. Marsala-laced creams, egg creams and cooking liqueurs may still have a market, but they can hardly contribute to the profile of what should really be a niche product.

Today it is encouraging to see signs that Marsala, the wine, is finally emerging from such oenological ignominy. Marco De Bartoli has blazed the trail by dissociating himself from the very term, preferring instead to call his superb traditional *vino liquoroso* "*Vecchio Samperi*". As a result, growing awareness on the part of discerning drinkers of what Marsala could and should be is opening up a potential market for promising young producers such as Domenico Buffa.

What the courageous and determined few have shown is that really good Marsala actually transcends the concept of "dessert" or "sweet" wines. Lovingly made in small quantities from premium ingredients, such Marsalas take a long time to evolve. Like the finest French Cognac, they are for contemplative enjoyment. Moreover, they are surprisingly versatile, accompanying mature cheeses and even chocolate remarkably well.

⋂ *The nucleus of the historic Florio premises opposite the port in Marsala. The baglio once covered an even larger area, now occupied by other wineries.*

↻ *Smaller casks at the Pellegrino cellars in Marsala.*

⋂ *The vineyards in winter at Contessa Entellina.*

While the golden Marsala must be made with Grillo, Catarratto, Damaschino or Inzolia grapes, its ruby counterpart derives from Pignatello, Nero d'Avola or Nerello Mascalese. With their 18% alcohol, the finest Marsalas are the dry, almost nutty Vergine, which must be aged in wooden casks for at least 5 years, and the Vergine Stravecchio or Riserva, which requires ageing for at least 10 years. To fortify them producers use fine grape spirit, or the Solera method, which involves blending different vintages, so that a certain amount of the younger wine is gradually mixed with older, stronger wines of the same provenance. This latter method allows for continuity and persistence of aromas over a period of twenty years, or more.

Marsala, the town, offers plenty of opportunity for visiting historic wineries where huge wooden casks still cradle the precious liquid on which past fortunes were built: Florio, still impressive in scale though somewhat touristy; Pellegrino, with its magnificent ageing cellar; Cantine Rallo, who now focus largely on table wines.

Indeed, over the past few years many of Marsala's winemakers have made table wines their core activity. Even Pellegrino, a company that remains true to its original vocation with Marsala still accounting for 40% of its business, now also produces some excellent table wines under the Duca di Castelmonte label. Foremost among these in undoubtedly the full-bodied *Gorgo Tondo IGT*, a Nero d'Avola/Cabernet Sauvignon blend.

Though it no longer produces Marsala, the Rallo family's Donnafugata winery is one of the most dynamic and diversified in the area. With its 230 hectares of vineyard at Contessa Entellina, in the Belice valley southeast of Marsala, it produces a wide range of wines of character and elegance, as well as a Passito and a Moscato from grapes grown on the island of Pantelleria.

The Rallos have been involved in viticulture in the area for five generations, and were (as the name suggests) once owners of the prominent Cantine Rallo. This now belongs to the Vesco brothers, Francesco and Andrea, whose vineyards are largely located northeast of Marsala on the hillsides near Alcamo. Great care goes

⋒ *Night harvesting at Donnafugata's Contessa Entellina estate has attracted considerable media attention.*

➲ *Nino Galfano, the oenologist at the Baglio Hopps winery, and the casks he favours for fermenting and ageing the excellent Baglio Hopps Grillo white wine.*

➲➲ *Training noses and palates: a tasting session for students of winemaking and viticulture at the Agricultural Institute in Marsala.*

into making the three Marsalas (*Fine*, *Superiore* and *Vergine*), with ageing in Slavonian oak that is protracted well beyond the minimum duration specified by the DOC. Yet this currently amounts to a mere 400,000 bottles a year, as opposed to the 1.600,000 bottles of fine table wines, most of them extremely persuasive single varietals.

A similar focus on fine table wines is also a feature of the Baglio Hopps winery, founded in 1811 by Englishman James Hopps and currently run by his descendents, Giacomo and Fabio Hopps. The grapes for the three red wines are grown at an altitude of 150–200 metres near Mazara del Vallo, whereas as those for the whites, including an impressive *Grillo*, come from vineyards located higher up in the vicinity of the winery's new headquarters, in a renovated baglio just off the road leading east from Marsala towards Salemi. Out of respect for the past, the two Marsalas produced by the winery bear the name James Hopps on the label, whereas the three white and the three red table wines are labelled Baglio Hopps.

The attention paid to fine table wines by companies once devoted exclusively to Marsala is proof of the town's dynamism, its ability to redefine its vocation. Considerable stimulus must have derived from the transfer from Palermo to Marsala of the Regional Institute for Viticulture and Wine's experimental winery. Moreover, the recently founded degree course in Viticulture and Oenology is gradually supplying the area – indeed the island – with a flow of well-trained youngsters. It is thus not surprising to discover that the *Strada del Vino di Marsala*, the local Wine Route, is well established, with six intelligent itineraries already mapped out and an informative booklet to accompany them. Moreover, there is at least one restaurant in the area (Bacco's in Via Trieste 5) that hosts tasting events in which the menu is designed to accompany the wines. All this suggests that Marsala, both the wine and the town, are ready for a comeback.

Gorgo Tondo – Duca di Castelmonte

Cantine Pellegrino

IGT – red wine. The Nero d'Avola is aged in large barrels; the Cabernet Sauvignon for 6 months in wooden casks and barriques

Nero d'Avola 60%, Cabernet Sauvignon 40%

4–5 years

Plenty of berries and cooked plums on the nose; fruity and rounded in the mouth, with a slightly stringent finish

Game, roasted red meats, mature hard cheese

Gruali

Cantine Rallo

IGT – white wine aged for 8 to 9 months in barriques

Grillo 100%

2 years

Hints of fresh herbs, vanilla and orange blossom on the nose; full-bodied and harmonious in the mouth, with a distinct note of almond paste and a long aromatic finish

Pork, rabbit, chicken, goat's milk cheese, fresh tuna or swordfish

The South West:
Menfi, Agrigento, Licata

Towards the Temples

Once one of the most prosperous of the Greek cities in Sicily, Agrigento is now the capital of one of the poorest provinces in Italy. Crowning a narrow ridge overlooking the valley, the medieval and modern city occupies the site of the ancient acropolis and encroaches painfully on the classical ruins located to the seaward below. To add to its problems, much of the province has to put up with a hot, arid climate and a chronic shortage of water. The inland areas northeast of Agrigento appear parched beyond belief even in winter, their townsfolk somehow coping with piped water supplied once every two weeks.

It may thus come as a surprise to discover that this south-western coastal area with its inland hillsides is the island's second most important province for viticulture. Happily, most of the excellent wine produced in the province of Agrigento does not end up in blends concocted elsewhere, but is bottled and sold as quality IGT and DOC table wines.

Though it is the cooperative wineries that produce the bulk of these wines, processing a good 30% of the island's grape output,

there are also a number of small and medium-sized wineries that in recent years have shown admirable entrepreneurial spirit in their production and marketing of fine wines. Indeed, the province boasts two wineries whose acclaim has spread so far afield in recent years that they have indirectly played a major role in forging the newfound perception of Sicilian viticulture as a whole. Though one is a family company and the other a large cooperative, the two are actually related, and not only because they both hail from the same north-western reach of the province.

Their point of contact is Diego Planeta, a gentleman of extraordinary energy and foresight with family property in the provinces of Agrigento, Ragusa and Siracusa. On his estates he oversaw the transformation of traditional sharecrop farming into a modern agricultural business with 120 employees and a focus on high quality wines and olive oil.

This is, however, only one aspect of Diego Planeta's ongoing contribution to the island's oenolgical excellence. In 1964, at the age of 24, he was one of the founding members of the Cantine Settesoli, the Menfi-based cooperative winery that is the largest of its sort in Italy, and one of the largest in Europe. Since 1972 he has also been its chairman, assuring that its primary focus continues to be quality. The winery's team of 6 agronomists provide the associated growers with constant advice pertaining to all aspects of viticulture, and the finest grapes grown in the 6500 hectares of vineyard thus controlled go into Settesoli's excellent Mandrarossa label.

With so much going on it is hard to imagine how Diego Planeta also found time to preside over the Palermo-based *Istituto Regionale della Vite e del Vino*. Yet under his chairmanship from 1985 to 1992 the institution enjoyed its most dynamic years, establishing secondary offices in Alcamo, Marsala, Milazzo and Noto, setting up a couple of hundred experimental vineyards throughout the island, and furthering such empirical research in the Institute's experimental winery.

Merlot	
🏠	Planeta
🍾	IGT – red wine aged for 12 months in French oak barrels
🍇	Merlot 100%
⏱	8–10 years
🍷	Intensely fruity aromas in which plum and mulberry prevail, followed by spicy tones with a touch of ginger, mint, vanilla and coffee. Rich and velvety in the mouth, with elegant tannins and long, aromatic persistence
🍴	Mature cheeses, cheese pasta timbale, meat stews

Furetta	
🏠	Mandrarossa
🍾	IGT – white wine fermented and aged for 8 months in barriques
🍇	Grecanico 60%, Chardonnay 40%
⏱	5–6 years
🍷	Vanilla and exotic fruits on the nose; full in the mouth, with a long finish ending with persistent notes of banana, pineapple and lychee
🍴	Dishes based on fish or white meats

Gigantic fermentation tanks at the Settesoli cooperative winery at Menfi.

Models for Development

Both the Planeta and the Settesoli headquarters are located at Menfi, where vineyards occupy a wide swathe of land overlooking the sea that until the 1950s was largely devoted to cereal and artichoke farming. Planeta started its replanting programme in 1985, and since then has continued to expand with extraordinary skill and prescience under the management of Diego Planeta's offspring, Francesca and Santi, and his nephew Alessio. The young Planeta cousins must have inherited considerable gifts from their father/uncle, since they seem to embody a rare combination of expertise, dynamism, culture and fun. The wines they produce are of such reliable excellence that Planeta was recently included in Wine Spectator's list of the world's hundred best wineries.

The Planeta winery at Menfi comprises five hectares of Syrah cultivated in a mild, hilly area with red, sandy soils not far from the sea. In the same district there are a further 23 hectares of Fiano and Chardonnay whose aromatic potential is brought to the fore by soils that are rich in clay and chalk. The Menfi winery is used for vinifying and ageing the red wines. The whites, on the other hand, are made at the winery occupying a handsome 16th century *baglio* located further inland, near Sambuca di Sicilia, a charming town founded by the Arabs early in the 9th century. Naturally protected from the scirocco winds typical of the coast, the vineyards sloping down towards the Lago Arancio are planted with Chardonnay, Merlot, Grecanico, Nero d'Avola, Sauvignon Blanc and Fiano; higher up, where the grapes ripen later, a further 28 hectares were planted in 1999 with Cabernet Franc, Merlot, Syrah, Petit Verdot and a little Pinot Noir. The idea is to take advantage of the different types of soil on the hill by growing several red grape varieties with a view to producing a single great wine from a single vineyard.

Planeta also has vineyards producing Cerasuolo di Vittoria DOC in the province of Ragusa and a recently completed winery and

vineyards near Noto, in Siracusa province. Yet despite owning vineyards in excess of 300 hectares, the company image is that of a perfectly tuned and contained family concern whose pursuit and achievement of quality has opened up new vistas for Sicilian viticulture in general. No wonder, therefore, that Planeta has had cult status practically thrust upon it (to seek cult status would hardly be in their style).

Cantine Settesoli is an entirely different operation, at least from the logistical point of view. Though it began with a mere 5 cooperative members who together owned 100 hectares of vineyard, over a period of thirty years it has expanded to encompass just over 2300 growers with an average of 2 hectares of vineyard each, the fruit of which goes into the production of 12 million bottles a year. On such a scale, advising growers on where to plant what, how to prune and when to pick, then programming the arrival of the ripe grapes in the three main winery facilities so that vinification can proceed in ideal conditions is a major and

complex organizational feat. It has also been an educational accomplishment, since more and more growers are now opting for quality over quantity.

The winery, in fact, produces two distinct lines: the Settesoli wines, which include the Porta Palo and Torre Solada reds, whites and rosés destined for supermarket distribution (the name Inycon is used for export), and the fine quality Mandrarossa label that set out in 1999 to make a name for itself in good restaurants and *enoteche*. Having already met with widespread acclaim, including numerous Seals of Approval from the International Wine Challenge and Gold Medals from Vinitaly, the Mandrarossa output is destined to expand in coming years as increasing numbers of growers are able to supply the quality grapes such wines require.

The Mandrarossa line includes a number of interesting blends, three international varietals and three wines made from local or nearly local grape varieties: a Nero d'Avola, a Grecanico and, since 2002, a Fiano. As Planeta has already shown with its *Cometa IGT*,

Santa Cecilia		Bendicò	
🏠	Planeta	🏠	Cantine Settesoli - Mandrarossa
🍷	IGT – red wine aged for 12 months in French oak	🍷	IGT – red wine whose components are aged separately for 14 months in barriques
🍇	Nero d'Avola 100%	🍇	Nero d'Avola 60%, Merlot 30%, Syrah 10%
🕐	8–10 years	🕐	6–8 years
🍷	Complex nose with berries, pepper, clove, carob, vanilla. Smooth, warm, full-bodied and yet fresh in the mouth, with developing tannins	🍷	Elegantly fruity, slightly austere, with a long, intriguing finish
🍴	Chestnut soup; flavoursome meat dishes, including lamb; beef couscous; mature cheese	🍴	Red meats and semi-seasoned cheeses

↑ *View of the Planeta vineyards over looking Lago Arancio, near Sambuca di Sicilia.*

⊃ *The Planeta cellars and part of the vineyards near Lago Arancio.*

Fiano, which originally came from around Avellino in the Campania region, does well in this area, producing wines that are elegant, aromatic and long on the palate.

In the Wake

Today there are various wineries producing wines that are not only correct, but also interesting, located within the triangle delineated by S. Margherita di Belice, Sambuca di Sicilia and Menfi. Though soil, climate and local entrepreneurship all obviously play a part in what these wineries are achieving, there can be no doubt that, in different ways, their paths have been lit by the dazzling flares sent up in recent years by Planeta, and indeed Settesoli.

The Cantina Sociale Corbera is located at S. Margherita di Belice, the Cantina Sociale Cellaro at Sambuca di Sicilia: both of these cooperative wineries make reliable to good reds and whites. Among the smaller wineries that could make a name for themselves in coming years there is Monte Olimpo at Sambuca di Sicilia and Baglio San Vincenzo at Menfi. By contrast, the Feudo Arancio estate near Sambuca di Sicilia recently purchased and entirely replanted by the Mezzacorona group from Trento in northern Italy is huge in scale. It is still early days to judge the wines. For the present, this property simply goes to show that the winegrowing potential of the area has been recognized by major business-orientated wine concerns who perceive their Sicilian investments as a *fiore all'occhiello*, or badge of excellence.

Menfi, Sambuca di Sicilia and Santa Margherita di Belice all actually have their own DOCs, established between 1995 and 1996. Like many of the less significant Sicilian appellations they are somewhat comprehensive in their span. Yet though most of the fine wines produced in the area present themselves as IGTs, it may well be that the presence of the DOCs can be read as a slow return to optimism on the part of populations sorely afflicted by the atrocious earthquake of 1968.

♠ The laboratory at the Settesoli winery at Menfi provides the wine technicians with constant feedback during all stages of winemaking.

⮑ A view of old buildings at Sambuca di Sicilia, the small hilltop town overlooking one of the Planeta estates.

⮑ The courtyard of the Baglio San Vincenzo, near Menfi.

⮑ The old palmento, or wine cellar, at Baglio San Vincenzo is now part of the dining room in the restaurant attached to the winery.

To travel the inland area thirty years ago was to see and touch and breathe despondency. Today, S. Margherita di Belice may appear to be a slightly soulless town still attached to the visible traces of an earlier way of life, yet it also expresses a certain energy. The sensation is that there is a growing awareness of the value of quality agriculture: olive oil, prickly pears, cheese making, and most importantly wine. The newly founded Wine Route of the Terre Sicane involves the three towns mentioned above, plus Montevago, whose hot springs have got off to a new start at the Terme Acqua Pia. With avowed support from Planeta, Settesoli, and a number of the less prominent wineries, this Strada del Vino should become one of the island's most active and attractive in coming years.

Ancient Lands, New Wineries

Sciacca, a little south east of Menfi, now also has its own DOC and can offer an enticing mixture of archaeology from the stunning Selinunte site, wine and hot springs. One of the most interesting wineries is Miceli, which also has magnificent old cellars on the island of Pantelleria, where the focus is naturally on the local Passito and Moscato. At its Sciacca headquarters, Miceli produces some fine table wines, the top end of which includes an enjoyable *Nero d'Avola*.

For the present, however, the wines of the Sciacca area are for the most part rather like members of a more than presentable chamber choir. For the great solo voices of Sicily's new oenology the place to head for is the triangle created by Agrigento, Licata and the inland city of Caltanissetta, just beyond the provincial border. This is an area that in the late 19th century employed some 16,000 miners, many of them young women and children, to extract sulphur manually from an average depth of 60 metres. Though this gave Italy a world monopoly of sulphur by 1900, it did so at the cost of atrocious working conditions. The last mines in the province of Agrigento were closed down in 1988, and the local economy has scarcely rallied since

♩ *Winter pruning aims at reducing the number of buds, so that new growth is contained and greater vigour goes into the formation of the fruit.*

Nero d'Avola	
🏠	Miceli
🍾	IGT – red wine aged for 12 months in barriques, 6 months in vats and 6 months in the bottle
🍇	Nero d'Avola 100%
⏱	4–5 years
🍷	Good balance of fruit, vanilla and spices on the nose; fresh and rounded in the mouth, with elegant tannins
🍴	Red meats, game, mature cheeses

Nero d'Avola	
🏠	Morgante
🍾	IGT – red wine aged for 4 months in barriques
🍇	Nero d'Avola 100%
⏱	3–6 years
🍷	Red berries and plums on the nose; rounded, balanced and full in the mouth, with a sustained, elegant finish
🍴	All meat dishes, including pasta, mature cheeses, grilled vegetables

then. Viticulture in this area is hard work, and the concept that quality will ultimately pay is at pains to gain acceptance.

It is very much the message at the Morgante winery, however. The estate is located just outside Grotte, a small town with, for this area, a uniquely thriving economy based on the wholesale import of rugs from the Middle East and, even more strangely given the climate, fur coats. While neighbouring towns languish for lack of employment and the severity of the torrid, dry climate, Grotte is full of enterprise. And so is the surrounding countryside, at least partly thanks to the vision of Antonio Morgante and his sons Carmelo and Giovanni. The family first decided to make their own wines with the grapes grown in their vineyards in 1994. Three years later Riccardo Cotarella, one of Italy's foremost oenologists, visited the area and agreed to act as consultant to the winery. Since then, Morgante has become a point of reference for Nero d'Avola.

The 200-hectare family estate consists of almond orchards and vineyards planted in clayey, calcareous soils at 450 to 550 metres above sea level, just 25 kilometres from the Valley of the Temples. Though they have also planted a little Merlot and Cabernet Sauvignon, the focus is Nero d'Avola, "whose main defect is its versatility", says Carmelo Morgante with a wry smile. "Here we are constantly in drought conditions. If you give Nero d'Avola water, it will produce a lot, but not quality. We almost hate it, like you do a singularly tiresome relation".

Though coaxing this particular family member into behaving appropriately must be a constant battle in such a dry climate, the bottled outcome is admirable. Morgante makes just two wines, and of these the *Don Antonio Nero d'Avola* made from the fruit of low-yielding vineyards planted in the early 1970s has rightly been awarded the coveted Three Glasses accolade.

Another example of local individuality in winemaking can be seen in the modus operandi and products of Le Botti di Antistene winery. It was set up in 1998 by three farmers from the town of Racalmuto, otherwise renowned as the birthplace of Leonardo Sciascia, one of

Insolia	Don Antonio	Rosso della Noce
Feudo Principi di Butera	Morgante	Le Botti di Antistene
IGT – white wine aged in steel vats	IGT – red wine aged for 12 months in barriques and 6 months in the bottle	IGT – red wine aged for 12 months in oak casks
Inzolia 100%	Nero d'Avola 100%	Nero d'Avola 100%
2 years	6-8 years	5 years at least
Exotic fruits and broom blossom on the nose; full, harmonious palate with hints of almond	Ripe red fruits, spices and deep chocolaty aromas; remarkably full-bodied in the mouth, sensual yet disciplined, memorably persistent	Plenty of black currant and a hint of chocolate on the nose; great balance in the mouth, with full-bodied ripe fruit and a lovely long finish
Seafood, chicken, vegetable pasta dishes	Game, red meats, mature cheeses	Red meat, mature hard cheese

the greatest Italian writers of the 20th century. Wishing to make wines with their own select grapes, but as yet unable to build cellars of their own, the enterprising Calogero (Lillo) Sardo and his partners sought the oenological consultancy of the excellent Bambina and Centonze team and rented space from a neighbouring cooperative winery that had fallen on hard times and closed down. Their *Rosso della Noce* barrel aged Nero d'Avola is an admirable achievement. Slightly further east are two consolidated wineries operating commercially on a different scale. One is Milazzo, a well established family concern located northeast of Campobello di Licata on a plateau ten kilometres inland, at an altitude of 370-400 metres, where the temperature drops considerable at night. The Milazzo family turned to quality wine making in the 1970s, and is aided in this pursuit by oenologist Cesare Ferrari from Franciacorta in Lombardy, an area renowned for its sparkling wines. With such input Milazzo is one of the few Sicilian wineries to produce Metodo Classico (meaning Champagne style) sparkling wines using a

blend of Inzolia and Chardonnay, as well as red blends that favour Sicilian grape varieties, the barrel-aged *Maria Costanza Nero d'Avola* with its lingering hints of liquorice, and several white blends based on Inzolia, Catarratto and Chardonnay.

Between the towns of Riesi and Licata is the important and commercially well-placed Feudo Principi di Butera winery, once an agricultural estate belonging to the aristocratic Branciforti and Lanza di Scalea dynasties and now the property of the Zonin family that hails from the Veneto. Some years ago Zonin was a name that conjured up images of ordinary flagon wine, but in recent years Gianni Zonin has gradually been expanding and investing in the sort of quality that enhances prestige. He now has significant wineries in Friuli, Lombardy, Piedmont, Tuscany and Puglia as well as Sicily, to say nothing of his Barboursville Vineyards in Virginia, USA.

Closer to Licata are two other wineries that embody the positive individualism that seems to be typical of this area. Tenuta Barone

ᘯ *The early spring landscape between Sciacca and Agrigento, with a view of the sea in the distance.*

➲ *Almond trees in bloom near Grotte. Nero d'Avola and almonds prosper in similar soils and climates.*

ᘯ *The landscape of the inland areas of southwestern Sicily seems to speak for the hardships suffered by its inhabitants in early modern times.*

🎧🎧 *Summer heat reverberates from the stony soils on the Quignones estate near Licata.*

➲ *The vibrant green of the vineyards constrasts with the beige of sun-baked soils in the area around Licata.*

Sympòsyo - Grecanico Chardonnay

🏠 Le Botti di Antistene

🍾 IGT – white wine, the Chardonnay aged for 40 days in barriques, and the blend for a further 4 months in the bottle

🍇 Grecanico 70%, Chardonnay 30%

🍷 2 years

🍷 An elegant wine with the right balance of fresh fruit, citrus leaves and a touch of spice

🍴 Pasta dishes, white meats, tasty fish

Nicolò La Lumia lies in a plain where summers are uncompromisingly hot, winters are mild and autumns warm and sunny. In keeping with its ancient lineage, the La Lumia family only grows the historic local grape varieties, conserving a number of vines planted in sandy soils that escaped the phylloxera onslaught of the early 20th century. The *Don Totò* Nero d'Avola, so named in honour of the ancestor who first bottled wine on the estate and contributed to the modernization of its agriculture in general, is a fine wine made in very limited quantities that has convinced wine critics far and wide that Sicily's current wine renaissance is no transitory phenomenon. Singular among the winery's products is also the *Nikao* passito wine made from raisined Nero d'Avola.

On a sun-baked hillside just across the valley from the La Lumia estate is what the Italians call *una realtà emergente* in the firmament of Sicilian wine. While the Aziende Agricole Quignones has been growing grapes for many years, it only decided to make and bottle its own wines some fifteen years ago. Under the guidance of Marsala-based oenologist Luciano Parrinello, it has wisely taken the time it needed to go public with its products. And the outcome vindicates the wait: the *Castel San Giacomo* blend of Nero d'Avola, Cabernet Sauvignon and Merlot is elegant, balanced, rich in spicy fruit without being heavy; and the *Tenuta d'Apaforte Nero d'Avola* whose 1998 vintage won a Gold Medal in Brussels in 2003 has attractive blackcurrant aromas and pleasantly soft tannins.

It may be that winemakers who live in such close proximity with important vestiges of a distant past are more inspired by their own immediate landscape than they are by fashion. For the fact is that the winemakers of the Agrigento province stand out as individuals, as producers who care little for trends but are particularly sensitive to every nuance of the soil and microclimate that are their heritage. Though the days of building temples are long gone, they are still able to honour the oenological tradition derived from their Hellenic forebears.

Nero d'Avola Tenuta d'Apaforte

Quignones

IGT – red wine aged for 12 months in barriques, then 6 months in the bottle

Nero d'Avola 100%

4-5 years

Fine nose with plenty of berries, pepper, a hint of chocolate; full-bodied in the mouth, with elegant tannins and sustained finish

Red meats, game, mature cheese

Nikao

La Lumia

IGT – red raisin wine aged for at least two years in steel and a further 12 months in the bottle

Nero d'Avola 100%

10 years at least

Prunes, dried figs, marzipan on the nose; extraordinary dry entry in the mouth, followed by rich raisined fruit that caresses the palate, and ending in a long, dry finish

Almond biscuits, apple tart, mature hard cheeses

Don Totò

La Lumia

IGT – red wine matured in steel for 2 years and then in barriques for a further 6 months

Nero d'Avola 100%

At least 10 years

Full of fruit and depth on the nose; imposingly full-bodied in the mouth

Roasted red meats, game, mature hard cheeses

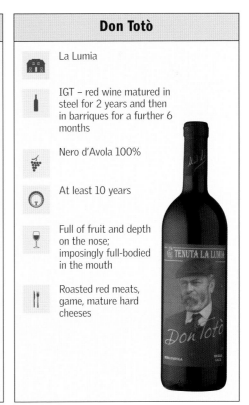

The South East:
Vittoria, Ragusa,
Noto, Siracusa

Baroque Elegance

The south-eastern provinces of Sicily embrace towns whose names have long been linked with viticulture: Cerasuolo di Vittoria, which came into being in the early 1600s when the city itself was founded; Nero d'Avola, Sicily's quintessential red grape variety that has spread from this area through much of the island; Moscato di Noto and Moscato di Siracusa, thought to descend from the Biblino and Pollio wines admired by the writers of Antiquity. When Paolo Balsamo, a well-informed observer, visited Sicily in the early 1800s, he declared this area to produce "table wines of great credit, indeed in my opinion the best in the whole island".

The same area also boasts some of the finest baroque architecture in southern Europe, recently recognised as a UNESCO World Heritage site. It arose following the disastrous earthquake of 1693, and shows a degree of pride and optimism that not even a calamitous act of god could fully undermine. While baroque architecture elsewhere in Europe may now appear top-heavy and somewhat bombastic, here in southeastern Sicily it is a well-tempered style that delights in curious ornament while maintaining

a sense of measure. It is thus both inventive and harmonious.

The epithet also applies to the wines. While belonging to the same southernmost tip of the island, they differ considerably from one area to the next. Yet though they comprise diverse reds and whites, ranging from distinctive table to dessert wines, the general hallmark is elegance, plus a gratifying element of *divertimento*.

The landscape surrounding much of the winegrowing areas in the provinces of Ragusa and Siracusa features white dry-stone walls that cover entire hillsides in a startling, lacy geometrical embrace. Pale, craggy spurs of the same stone jut from the ground, while the calcareous substratum forms numerous caves that once served as stables, mills, dwellings and in some cases even places of worship for the local populations. Vineyards are interspersed with olive groves, citrus orchards and pasturelands. Outlined against the terse blue sky are carob trees whose dark green foliage sheds deep pools of shade among the dazzling light. The dramatic chiaroscuro characteristic of the area has inspired photographers of the calibre of Giuseppe Leone and the painters collectively known as the Scicli Group, most notably Piero Guccione.

The Cerasuolo Triangle

When Vittoria Colonna Henriquez, Countess of Modica, founded the city of Vittoria in 1607, she endowed the first 75 farmers to settle there with a hectare of land each, on condition that they plant a further hectare with vines. Ever since, the principal grape varieties grown here have been Nero d'Avola and Frappato. This combination of strength and elegance, structure and aroma, "plum" and "cherry", is what makes Cerasuolo di Vittoria DOC such an inviting wine.

The permitted production area for Cerasuolo di Vittoria actually stretches over a fairly widespread area of the provinces of Catania, Ragusa and Caltanissetta. However, the premium producers largely revolve around the triangle created by Vittoria, Comiso and Chiaramonte Gulfi, which includes the wide Acate valley.

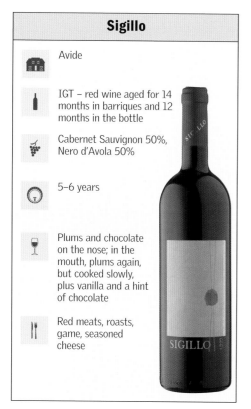

Sigillo	
🏠	Avide
🍾	IGT – red wine aged for 14 months in barriques and 12 months in the bottle
🍇	Cabernet Sauvignon 50%, Nero d'Avola 50%
⏱	5–6 years
🍷	Plums and chocolate on the nose; in the mouth, plums again, but cooked slowly, plus vanilla and a hint of chocolate
🍴	Red meats, roasts, game, seasoned cheese

☊ *The church of Saint John the Baptist in Vittoria.*

Seen from the ridge above, this lower lying area appears like a broad river of green that draws a gentle breeze in its wake. While the soils on the ridge are clayey, further down they become sandier, reddish in hue and friable, with an underlying layer of tuff stone that maintains the water balance in the vine. Since such loose soils do not retain the heat absorbed during the day, there is a marked difference in temperature at night, and this contributes to the unique character and good acidity of the Frappato. Where the clay component is stronger, a number of producers prefer to leave the newly planted rootstock for a year to get established before grafting on the desired grape variety. This may mean losing a year in terms of grape production, but it makes up for it in precocious quality.

Between 1997 and 1998, Planeta, which so often heralds future tendencies in Sicilian winemaking, set up its "DOC project" aimed at producing wines with a distinct regional identity. This meant planting Nero d'Avola and Frappato on 17 hectares of land in the Dorilli family property near Acate. The first vintage was 2001, produced in small steel vats specially designed for the vinification of a wine to be drunk young, when its characteristic freshness is at its most inviting.

Not far from here is the Valle dell'Acate winery, once a small cooperative structure and now the property of six partners led by Giuseppe Jacono and his daughter Gaetana, known as Tana, a bright light in the small but select firmament of female winemakers in Sicily. Because the winery itself was built to accommodate bulk production, the existing equipment had to be adapted when the focus became fine bottled wines. Instead of discarding the huge steel fermentation vats, they were simply cut down to size. These tanks are now open topped, a virtue born of necessity: "We weren't in a position to throw out what we had there and start all over again", explains Tana. "With this system we stir the lees manually, and this helps the extraction of polyphenolics from the skins".

The Valle dell'Acate winery has a truly magnificent tasting venue made out of the ground floor of an impressive two-storey *palmento*, or winemaking facility dating back to the first years of the 1900s. The blended wines are aged in barriques, while the three varietals (Inzolia, Nero d'Avola and Frappato) are aged in steel, so that they speak entirely for themselves with no prompting from wood. The excellent *Cerasuolo di Vittoria DOC* is a classic 60/40% blend of Nero d'Avola and Frappato, with the Nero d'Avola aged in barriques for 8 to 9 months. Tana thinks that in future years they may switch to larger barrels for this particular wine. An enchanting achievement is also Il *Frappato IGT*, made, as the name suggests, entirely with the Frappato grape variety, and thus something of a rarity. It is a wine of minuet-like elegance made for immediate enjoyment.

Located due east of Vittoria, just outside Comiso, the Avide winery is another quality producer currently seeing the fruits of vineyard renewal and modernisation in the winery. Hard winter and spring pruning of trellised alberello-trained vines have reduced grape yields to a satisfactory average of 1.5 kilos per plant. The result is a range of fine wines that includes the rightly acclaimed barrique-aged *Barocco Cerasuolo di Vittoria DOC* (60% Frappato, 40% Nero d'Avola), and the raspberry-nosed *Etichetta Nera Cerasuolo di Vittoria DOC* made with an 80/20%

Il Frappato

Valle dell'Acate

IGT – red wine aged for 6 months in steel tanks and 3 months in the bottle

Frappato 100%

To be drunk young

Fragrant fresh fruit, with distinct notes of bilberry, blackberry, raspberry; in the mouth, bright, fresh berries, yet light and unexpectedly persistent

Starters with seasoned and fresh cheeses, cold cuts and game pâté, fish, especially prawns, if served chilled at 12-13°

➲ *Prickly pears are cultivated for their fruit in southern Sicily.*

blend of Frappato and Nero d'Avola that has an unexpectedly dry finish. Both of these wines should be enjoyed while still young, fresh and fruity. By contrast, the Sigillo blend of Cabernet Sauvignon and Nero d'Avola that has matured in barriques for 14 months and at least 12 in the bottle is a wine that will continue to evolve well after it has been released. Another attractive product is the Herea Inzolia varietal, whose aromas of banana and citrus lead up to a pleasantly dry, fresh finish.

The COS winery located just north east of Vittoria is the product of – and a tribute to – intelligent individualism. Giusto Occhipinti and Giambattista Cilia were still students of architecture in Palermo when they first made wine from grapes grown on Cilia's father's property. That was 1980, and their main goal was to have fun. The rest of the story is an ode to enjoyment.

The outcome of the first, highly empirical vintage was so promising that Cilia and Occhipinti found themselves bottling it for dispatch to a wine bar they both frequented in Palermo. In

due course a fine old *baglio* in the Pedalino district, between Vittoria and Comiso, was transformed into a winery that makes the necessary concessions to modernity, but looks with particular regard to tradition. Apart from the well-preserved vestiges of the original *palmento*, there is now also a room devoted to the fermentation and ageing of Nero d'Avola in 450-litre terracotta urns. The inspiration for this came from studies of winemaking in Sicily in Antiquity. And the results have proved interesting, revealing a fine balance of mineral aromas and fruit (see pages 18–20).

The idiosyncratic architect winemakers continue to do things their own way, eschewing cultured yeasts, keeping an eye on the lunar cycle, basing most of their decisions on knowledge acquired during their own 25 years' experience rather than on outside expertise. They currently produce two excellent Cerasuolo di Vittoria DOCs: a smooth, full-bodied one with hints of spice made with 40% Frappato and 60% barrel-aged Nero d'Avola; and the lighter *Vastunaca*, an 80% Frappato and 20% Nero d'Avola blend.

As well as the Maldafrica Cabernet Sauvignon/Merlot blend, the COS wines also comprise two crus, the barrel-aged *Pojo di Lupo Nero d'Avola IGT* and the barrique-aged *Scyri Nero d'Avola IGT*. Fullness, elegance and length are their hallmarks. Cilia declares that "a Nero d'Avola from Vittoria takes two years to mature and then continues its ascent, whereas the same wine made from grapes grown around Pachino reaches its zenith after 18 months, then begins its downwards trajectory". This is, of course, more a provocative homage to his own district than a vindicated scientific theory. As we shall see, there are now wines made with grapes grown in Pachino, Sicily's southernmost tip, that provide an eloquent rebuttal.

First, however, a visit to Chiaramonte Gulfi is required to complete the Cerasuolo triangle. Compared with the areas already mentioned, this landscape presents a hillier aspect, with vineyards planted between 400 and 500 metres above sea level and abundant olive groves. The soils are preponderantly calcareous and moderately clayey, and the temperature drops considerably at night, even at the height of summer. This latter factor lends the area

Il Moro

Valle dell'Acate

IGT – red wine aged in steel and then 9–12 months in the bottle

Nero d'Avola 100%

5–6 years

Slightly peppery on the nose; for the palate, plenty of fresh fruit and more elegance than muscle

Red meats, roast or stewed game, cheese, especially the locally made seasoned Ragusano added potential for white wines made with the local Albanello and Carricante grape varieties.

On hillsides caressed by a westerly breeze in the Roccazzo district, the small Poggio di Bortolone winery produces three Cerasuolo di Vittoria DOC consisting of different blends of Frappato and Nero d'Avola. So fresh and fair is the climate that the Cosenza family, who own the property, are able to cultivate their vines and olive groves in semi organic conditions. They also produce something of a curiosity for the area: Kiron, a Petit Verdot varietal that shows plenty of fresh, fruity promise.

The 25-hecatre Gulfi winery located at 500 metres altitude, just below the town of Chiaramonte Gulfi, is likely to become something of a cult producer in coming years. The property belongs to Vito Catania, a Milanese businessman whose family originally came from around Ragusa. Until 1996 Catania had sold his grapes to other wineries. Once he had decided to become a winemaker in his own right he summoned as a consultant oenologist Salvo Foti, whose deep knowledge and love of Sicilian flora and viticulture had already impressed Giuseppe Benanti on Mount Etna. With Foti's advice, Catania gradually extended his property to include a further 17 hectares in the neighbouring municipality of Licodia Eubea, and 30 hectares of Nero d'Avola in the prime growing areas of Pachino.

Foti is convinced that in Sicily the traditional self-supporting alberello vine, when densely planted, is the best system for producing quality grapes. However, it is notoriously labour intensive, and expert vinedressers are becoming a rare and expensive commodity. Vito Catania has thus seen fit to develop a mechanical planter and digger. This adaptation of a French *enjambeur*, the first of its sort in Sicily, has allowed the Gulfi winery to achieve a density of 8,500 trellised plants per hectare.

While Foti is clearly proud of this, he does not see it as the be all and end all. "You can export technology and grape varieties", he points out, "but you can't export the land". So the essence of the

Nerobufaleffi

🏠	Gulfi
🍷	IGT – red wine aged in small casks for at least a year and a few months in the bottle
🍇	Nero d'Avola 100%
🍷	5–6 years at least
🍷	Complex and intense on the nose, with berries, especially blackberries, and a little vanilla; elegant, fruity and harmonious in the mouth, with great persistence
🍴	Red meats, mature cheeses

Gulfi winery is particular respect for the individual characteristics of a given terroir and faith in the yeasts naturally present on the grape skins and in the winery. This has led to a focus on crus.

The Valcanzjria white comes from the Muti vineyard at Chiaramonte Gulfi, where different Chardonnay clones are cultivated alongside Carricante and Albanello, the local grape varieties that provide the wine with its acidity, complexity and ability to evolve over at least a couple of years. The Neromaccari and the Nerobufaleffi Nero d'Avolas respectively come from the Maccari and Bufaleffi vineyards located in the Pachino area, where the soils are very different (often within the same vineyard) and the arid climate produces high sugar concentrations in the grapes. It goes without saying that these two wines naturally distinguish themselves from the two excellent Nero d'Avolas produced up at Chiaramonte Gulfi. All four are elegant and balanced, but the length and breadth of the fruit of the Pachino wines is outstanding.

The Treasures of Noto

Located further south than the North African city of Tunis, Pachino is one aspect of a hugely promising future for winemaking in the vicinity of Noto. Built after the earthquake of 1693, Noto is considered the most charming and best preserved of the 18th century baroque cities of Sicily. As such, it is the most representative of the towns of the Valle del Barocco that in 2003 came under UNESCO tutelage.

Yet Noto is still a sleepy sort of place, almost unaware of what is happening all around it. Both the low-lying area of Pachino and the hilly district southwest of the town are currently attracting some major and discerning investment in vineyards and wineries. Sicilian winemakers of the calibre of Planeta, Vito Catania and Benanti, as well as Paolo Marzotto from the Veneto, and the Tuscans Filippo Mazzei (owner of Fonterutoli near Castellina in Chianti) and Antonio Moretti (Tenuta Sette Ponti in the province of Arezzo) have all

⋂ *Large wooden casks that are part of a museum housed in the historic cellars of the Valle dell'Acate winery.*

➲ *Recently planted vineyards, surrounded by centuries old olive trees.*

➲ *The Valle dell'Acate vineyards.*

realized that growing Nero d'Avola in its ur-location (Avola is just east of Noto) will produce wines that are distinctive, recognisably different from the Nero d'Avolas produced elsewhere on the island. With a little collective fine-tuning, this should give prominence to the hitherto somewhat insignificant Eloro DOC, the local appellation envisaging, among other things, a Nero d'Avola varietal. There is even a suggestion that in future it might change its name to the more easily identifiable "Val di Noto DOC".

Another interesting producer with vineyards in the chalky, clay-rich soils of Pachino is Antica Azienda Agraria Curto. The Curto family has farmed an estate that now straddles the provinces of Ragusa and Siracusa (until 1926 this was all Siracusa) since the late 1600s. Francesca Curto, who has piloted production towards quality wines, makes two very different Nero d'Avola varietals. *Curto Rosso IGT* is made from grapes grown in a 22 year old trellised vineyard due west and slightly south of Noto, near Ispica. It is full of berries, revealing a hint of liquorice to the nose, with a long, dry finish.

Curto Fontanelle, on the other hand, comes from alberello-trained vines planted in the friable, reddish-brown soils of Pachino 40 years ago. This vineyard produces less than a kilo of fruit per plant, and the grapes ripen a good ten days earlier in the extreme heat typical of the area. Aged briefly in barriques, the wine presents notable aromas of carob, which is a feature of Nero d'Avola grown in this area, and lovely rich fruit.

Francesca Curto, whose energy, foresight and charm bode well for winemaking with female input in Sicily, hopes in future years to produce Moscato di Noto as well. This is a project that Planeta has already brought to fruition at the new Noto winery. Located among gentle hills southwest of Noto, the aptly named Buonivini vineyards produce both Nero d'Avola and Moscato di Noto. Though the climate here is arid in the extreme, beneath the chalky white soil lies a layer of tuff stone that gradually releases the humidity sought by the roots of the vines, and indeed other plants. This explains the unexpected greenness of the landscape, even at the height of

↻ *Grafting the vines onto already planted root stock.*

➲ *Salvo Foti, oenologist at the Gulfi winery, as well as at Benanti on Mount Etna.*

➲↻ *Vineyards on the Gulfi estate near Chiaramonte Gulfi.*

➲➲ *Francesca Curto.*

summer, with carob, almond trees and vines all putting on a fine show of verdant defiance.

Though Moscato di Noto is considered a sweet dessert wine, Alessio Planeta's aim is to harvest the grapes before they are fully ripe, so that the wine conserves the desired acidity. Since Moscato di Noto has long been a forgotten genre, at least as far as quality wines are concerned, he feels that he has the freedom to reinvent the wine as his own fine nose and palate suggest. The outcome is thus more likely to be a wine for thoughtful sipping and matching that has greater versatility than most dessert wines as such. In the new Buonivini vineyards, a vertical trellis supports vines that

are pruned with a bilateral Guyot and spur cordon. "I simply don't believe that the alberello system produces the best quality grapes", declares Alessio Planeta. "The leaves are not spread out enough and all the grapes grow bunched up together". Admirers of Planeta's *Santa Cecilia Nero d'Avola IGT* will detect a gradual change in the wine's finer notes over recent years. This is due to moving from Menfi-grown grapes to a 50/50 blend of Menfi and Noto grapes between 2000 and 2002, and ultimately, as from the 2003 vintage, to grapes grown entirely in the Buonivini vineyards at Noto, where the carob and liquorice aromas are more pronounced.

Valcanzjria

Gulfi

IGT – white wine partly fermented in oak casks and aged for a few months in the bottle

Chardonnay 50%, Carricante 35%, Albanello 15%

2 years

Rich and intense on the nose, with hints of apple; dry and harmonious in the mouth, with pleasant acidity and a lingering undertone of anise and almond on the finish

Seafood in general

The Greek Heritage

The legendary Moscato di Siracusa dates back to the Greek colonization of the south east of Sicily in the 8th-7th centuries BC. It is said that the wine derives from the "Pollio Siracusano" obtained from sweet-smelling mature grapes harvested from a particular vine that was brought to the island from his native Thrace by King Pollium. Archestrato, the Sicilian writer of the 4th century BC who described in detail many of the island's culinary traditions, deemed the white Muscat wine of Syracuse to be particularly good because it does not lose its fragrance as it ages.

During the 19th century, Moscato di Siracusa was much appreciated throughout the western world, its fame culminating in a prize for excellence at the 1900 Paris exhibition. By the mid 20th century, however, output had begun to drop, reaching an all time low of around 4000 litres a year in 1999.

Happily the future of Moscato di Siracusa now looks more promising, largely thanks to the enterprise of Antonino (Nino) Pupillo. The Pupillo estates occupy a swathe of flattish land between the Ionian Sea, the Castello Eurialo and the walls built in the 4th century BC by Dionysius the Elder to defend the city of Syracuse, which under his rule became the most powerful city of Sicily and sovereign of the western Mediterranean.

Nino Pupillo first planted Moscato di Siracusa as part of an experimental vineyard monitored by the *Istituto Regionale della Vite e del Vino* in 1991. He now has 12 hectares of Moscato that produce three very different Moscato di Siracusa DOCs and a persuasive, aromatic dry white table wine, the *Cyane IGT*, released for the first time with the 2002 vintage and immediately snapped up by anyone lucky enough to have tasted it.

Full of aromas of exotic fruits and spices, the luscious *Solacium Moscato di Siracusa DOC* is made from Muscat grapes that are allowed to over-ripen on the vine. The *Pollio Moscato* is made with grapes that are only lightly withered on the vine before being crushed,

so that the wine is less sweet and well suited to accompanying certain cheeses. Likewise versatile is the somewhat spicy *Vigna di Mela Moscato*, a more complex wine that is aged in barriques.

Having hitherto made his wines in an anonymous modern building that is part of an industrial estate on the outskirts of Syracuse, Pupillo is currently restoring the splendid old family castle at the centre of the vineyards. This building dates back to the 13th century and has its own *palmento*, which is destined to become a tasting room once renovation is completed and the winery can move to its rightful home.

By the same token, after decades of neglect, the lovely promontory of Ortygia, once the centre of Syracuse when it was the largest and most beautiful city of the Greek world, is finally being restored. Many ancient monuments have been salvaged, the baroque architecture is regaining its former glory, and people are returning to live or holiday there. This suggests that the Moscato di Siracusa will also flourish in the wake of such rediscovered prosperity.

⋂ *Muscat grapes ready for harvesting in the Pupillo vineyards near Siracusa.*

⋂ *Part of a carved stone arch found on Nino Pupillo's historic family estate near Siracusa and now a symbol of the winery.*
⊂ *A section of the 13th century castle on the Targia estate near Siracusa that is currently being restored to house the Pupillo winery.*
⊂ ⊂ *Vineyards on the Planeta Buonivini estate near Noto.*

Cyane

🏠	Pupillo
🍾	IGT – white wine aged for 3 months in the bottle
🍇	Moscato bianco 100%
⏲	2 years at least
🍷	Extraordinarily aromatic and fragrant, with citrus blossom and fruit; curiously dry in the mouth, yet redolent of exotic fruits, jasmine and citrus
🍴	Fish and shellfish

The Volcano:
Mount Etna,
with a footnote on Messina

The Land of the Cyclopes

While several of Sicily's winegrowing areas may be surprising, Mount Etna is astounding. There is something magical, almost otherworldly about the idea of growing grapes within range of the natural pyrotechnics of a live volcano. And it is somehow humbling to realise that simple, microscopic lichens can take on the goliath of petrified lava, gradually preparing a bed for the wild fennel and broom that will take root and, over the centuries, help break down the rivers of dark rock until they become friable, mineral-rich soil.

Etnean viticulture is also singularly well established and relatively cohesive. This is partly due to the antiquity of viticulture on the slopes of the volcano. Often mentioned in Greek mythology, the wine of Mount Etna was judged by Cyclops, the legendary Homeric giant who resided in a cave on its slopes, to be "like nectar and ambrosia all in one". In fact it became his downfall. As "the huge monster" lay sleeping off the effects of plentiful drafts, Ulysses was able to drive a burning shaft into his one eye, and thus effect his escape.

The ancient presses still to be found in a number of Mount Etna's traditional *palmenti*, or wine cellars, correspond in detail to those described in the 3rd century BC by Cato, the Roman statesman, in his treatise *De agri cultura*. Designed along the same lines as olive presses, these towering structures featured "masts 2 feet thick, 11 feet high including tenons, with sockets cut out 3 feet long and 6 fingers wide beginning 1 foot from the ground" and "posts 2 feet thick, 12 feet high including tenons. Windlass 9 feet long plus tenons. Press-beam 25 feet long, including tongue 2 feet". While Etna's foremost commercial wineries now use modern pressing equipment, many of them have lovingly preserved these sturdy and ingenious witnesses to an important oenological past.

The fine houses that abound on the slopes of the Volcano also testify to the economic role of winemaking in the area in bygone centuries. The independent winegrowers who built them may have been smallholders or aristocratic landowners, or indeed members of the resident agricultural bourgeoisie that had emerged by the early 19th century. Each built according to his means, surrounding his property and shoring up his vineyards with well-constructed dry-stone walls made from blocks of lava removed from the terraced fields.

While most of pre-modern Sicily was divided into vast agricultural estates that were managed by agents for absentee landlords, farming on Etna was largely governed directly by the landowners who lived on the spot. This accounts for the reverence for what is local, the attention to detail, the continual improvements and the radical sense of belonging that are still tangible today.

Indeed, the presence of a time-honoured viticultural establishment may have indirectly dissuaded outside investment in wineries on the volcano, though doubtless the fear of molten lava has also played its part. There are exceptions, of course, including the small property comprising a hectare of vineyard recently purchased by Mick Hucknall, leader of the band Simply Red. But by and large winemakers from continental Italy ready to invest in Sicily have opted for other parts of the island.

Serra della Contessa

Benanti

Etna Rosso DOC – red wine aged in small casks for over one year, followed by 12 months in the bottle

Nerello Mascalese 90%, Nerello Cappuccio 10%

at least 3–4 years. Will become more austere with ageing

Subtle but intense on the nose, with a touch of wild berries, peach and fine wood. Full and harmonious in the mouth, with a long, quietly tannic finish

Red meats, wild fowl, mature cheese

➲ *Vines planted on narrow terraces shored up by volcanic stone walls at Valle Galfina on Mount Etna.*

Volcanic Energy

Founded in 1968, Etna DOC was Sicily's first wine appellation, and one of the earliest in Italy. Granted, the norms defined nearly 40 years ago could now do with some potentially divisive fine-tuning. Yet there is no doubt that the shared culture and aims of the foremost Etnean winegrowers have led them to go several steps beyond many of their counterparts elsewhere in Sicily in creating facilities and events that encourage wine tourism. Of these, by far the most important is the establishment in 2003 of the *Strada del Vino dell'Etna*, or Etna Wine Route. Under the dynamic chairmanship of Giuseppe Benanti, this organisation can count on public and private support in providing oenophiles with detailed guidelines to Etna's wine universe.

Heralding these developments, a number of wineries have turned buildings on their estates into accommodation for groups interested in the local food and wine. The Murgo Winery at Tenuta San Michele, near Santa Venerina, is a case in point. The beautifully located Tenuta Scilio di Valle Galfina, just beyond Linguaglossa, is currently following suit. And the Barone di Villagrande winery near Milo should soon have completed work on a B&B and a fine tasting venue located within the Nicolosi family's historic premises.

Moreover, a number of the charming small towns on the slopes of the volcano arrange annual festivities to do with wine and local gastronomy. Of these the most important is ViniMilo, a variety of tasting events, conferences and concerts held at Milo over a period of two weekends in early September. Another town whose dynamism belies its diminutive size is Sant'Alfio, located half way between the volcano and the old wine port of Riposto, on the coast. Like Milo and Viagrande, Sant'Alfio is a member of the Italy-wide Città del Vino association. Its three-day Etna Vini programme in November draws *appassionati* from far afield, luring them with tastings of local wines and gastronomy, and the chance to visit the town's nice little Museum of Vines and Wine. Likewise, the recently founded September wine festival at Santa Venerina, on the lower eastern slopes of the volcano, is also gaining widespread recognition, as is the annual wine conference held during the same month in Viagrande, just a few miles south.

Fire and Snow

Wineries on Mount Etna tend to be relatively small, which is due both to the agricultural history of the area and to the effort involved in clearing land interspersed with swathes of volcanic rock. Here and there, to one side of a verdant vineyard, a perfectly constructed black stone tower or pyramid is to be seen. It serves no purpose other than that of gathering in one orderly spot the volcanic stone that comes to the surface as the land is tilled. This amounts to turning a practical necessity into something beautiful; a tribute to an imposing landscape that the farmers of past generations chose to make.

Luxuriant in their growth, the vineyards that thrive on the rich soils and abundance of water occupy narrow terraces that follow the contours of the mountain, from the lower reaches of the foothills up to an altitude of 1000 metres above sea level. In winter, a mantle of snow covers not only the summit, but also the vine-clad slopes. In summer, a pinnacle of smoky vapour rising up from the main crater is

➲ *The Murgo winery's San Michele estate at Santa Venerina on Mount Etna.*

➲ *The geometry of terracing on Mount Etna at the Barone di Villagrande winery near Milo.*

clearly visible against the bright blue sky before it mingles with small, migrant clouds.

Although all the soils on the sides of Mount Etna are volcanic, they actually vary considerably from place to place. They may be formed by the breakdown of one or more different types of lava produced by eruptions dating back to different periods, and by eruptive material such as lapilli, ash and sand. As a result, in some areas the soils are very fine, while in others they contain a great deal of small pumice stones assuring such good drainage that no amount of seasonal rain will remain on the surface for long enough to form mud. This is important, since rainfall on the eastern slopes can reach 2,500 mm per year, most of it in autumn and winter, whereas the rest of the island is subject to drought. The volcanic soils of Etna are particularly rich in microelements (iron and copper), and fairly well endowed with potassium, phosphorus and magnesium. What they tend to lack is nitrogen and calcium.

Totally different from the prevailing atmospheric conditions of the rest of Sicily, the climate on Mount Etna also varies in relation to altitude and exposure. In the vine-growing areas, the average temperature is a good 14°C lower than that of the rest of the island. In the winter temperatures on the eastern slopes can drop as low as –4°C, and even when the vines begin to germinate in spring there is always the threat of a late freeze.

By the same token, given the altitude, in summer temperatures rarely go beyond 27°C. However, of particular significance for viticulture are the seasonal differences in temperature and the major drop in thermometer readings at night during the late spring and summer. This, along with the quality of light, influences the metabolism of the acids and the sugars of the grapes, thereby contributing to their overall quality.

The Growing Areas

There are three main areas for grape growing on Mount Etna. The first stretches from 400 to 900 metres altitude and faces east; the

Fiore di Villagrande

Barone di Villagrande

Etna Bianco DOC – white wine fermented on its yeasts in barriques for 6 months, and aged for several months in the bottle

Carricante 100%

3 years at least

Rich, intense aromas, with hints of apple; dry and harmonious in the mouth, with pleasant acidity and a lingering note of anice and almond

Fish

◖ *The Nicolosi family, owners of the Barone di Villagrande winery. From left to right, Carlo, Maria, Carla and Marco.*

➲ *Nerello Mascalese, the typical red grape variety of Mount Etna, growing happily on the Scilio estate at Valle Galfina.*

second, at an altitude of 400 to 800 metres, faces north; while the third, lying between 600 and 1000 metres altitude, enjoys a southerly exposure. Each can be said to have a particular vocation for distinctive wines.

For example, the finest growing area for the Carricante grape variety from which Etna Bianco Superiore is made is said to be east-facing Milo, where the Barone di Villagrande winery is located. Perched up at 750 metres and surrounded by woodland, this municipality comprises century-old vines that have survived in happy cohabitation with fruit trees and hazels. When vines are this old they produce limited quantities of premium fruit, which is nature's way of doing what man contrives to do by planting densely and pruning hard in his new vineyards.

A little lower down (400–500 m altitude) and slightly south of Milo is Viagrande, headquarters to the Benanti winery. In this and the neighbouring municipality the presence of extinct eruptive cones has provided the winemaker with vineyards that are very sheer and rich in

stony strata. This is proving to be an excellent sub-zone for low yields of superb quality Nerello Mascalese, which tends to ripen early in such conditions.

Benanti's *Serra della Contessa Etna Rosso DOC* is an eloquent case in point. It is produced from 100 year-old vines planted with a density of around 8000 vinestocks per hectare, which by today's standards is high. The must is kept on the skins for a protracted period, and following malolactic fermentation is transferred to casks for a year and then aged in the bottle for a further twelve months. This full-bodied, harmonious wine is remarkably long on the palate and will gain in elegance during three of four years of ageing.

Due north of Viagrande is Santa Venerina, home to at least 40 distilleries in the early 20th century and now largely synonymous with the Murgo winery. At the San Michele Estate, for over twenty years Emanuele Scammacca Barone del Murgo has been modernising the family winery and the 25 hectares of vineyard to produce wines of considerable aromatic complexity, including two sparkling wines made using the classic Champenois method, now something of a rarity for Sicily.

During the late 1800s, sparkling wines were made from grapes grown on the southern slopes of the volcano, near Biancavilla, by Barone Antonino Spitalieri di Muglia di Adrano, a farsighted local landowner whose winery represented the acme of viticultural modernity for the times. Alongside the indigenous Nerello Cappuccio, Nerello Mascalese and Carricante, he also introduced French grape varieties, focusing on the production of quality table wines. Today on this side of the mountain urbanisation has taken its toll and viticulture is much less important than it was a century ago, though it still plays a role within the municipality of Santa Maria Licodia.

Etna's finest red wines, made from the indigenous Nerello Mascalese grape variety, come from the northern slopes, where the vineyards are often interspersed with hazel orchards and the dark volcanic soils sometimes include patches of whitish earth derived from the non-volcanic hills across the valley rift. The best way to the view the countryside is to take the narrow-gauge Circumetnea railway that slowly snakes its way up and across the valley and foothills. Castiglione di Sicilia, Linguaglossa and Randazzo, all of them

members of the Città del Vino association, are well worth a visit.

The Tenuta Scilio organic winery lies on a little plateau of verdant, airy quietude at Valle Galfina, just outside Linguaglossa. The cellars and tasting facilities are fine examples of sensitive renovation and design, surrounded by a sea of greenery. They nestle in an area that has never been reached by the lava flows, and on the valley side the soils are rich with the humus that encourages vegetation. The vines thus require more radical spring and summer pruning. Within the Etna DOCs, the winery produces two excellent reds, a rosé and a white. It has also recently released a somewhat mysterious and thoroughly enchanting red dessert wine: *Sikelios*, made in small quantities from October-harvested grapes that are dried for three or four weeks prior to vinification.

If pressed on the subject of the grape variety from which Sikelios is made, engineer Giovanni Scilio will admit that on his property he discovered a self-made clone that he has managed to restore to productivity. The chances are that this apparently enigmatic vine is in fact an Alicante, or Grenache. Many hectares of this Pyrenean grape variety were indeed planted in the area during the early 1800s, at the behest of Horatio Nelson, the great English admiral whose naval activities in the Mediterranean won favour with Ferdinand IV, Sicily's Bourbon sovereign. As a token of his royal recognition he granted Nelson the Duchy of Bronte, whose estates included land in this area. A few of these vines may have been spared the phylloxera outbreak that destroyed so much of Sicilian viticulture during the late 19th and early 20th centuries.

This is certainly the case of the 30 hectares of Grenache found by Angelo Cesarò at the estate above Randazzo that his father purchased in 1967. The 170-hectare Gurrida property lies on a flood plain at an altitude of 850 metres on the northwest slopes of Etna, just across the rift from the Nebrodi range. At this altitude, the summer temperatures that can reach 30–35°C during the day will descend to around 12°C at night.

Scented broom abounds, with fruit trees, hazels and pasturelands

Orphéus	
🏠	Tenuta Scilio
🍾	Etna Rosso DOC – red wine aged for 12-14 months in oak (66% French, 33% American)
🍇	Nerello Mascalese 80%, Nerello Cappuccio 20%
⌚	At least 12 years
🍷	Complex nose with a fine balance of fruit and spice; in the mouth full, velvety and persistence, with fine tannins and excellent structure
🍴	Meaty pasta dishes, mushrooms, game and red meats

⌒ *Racks of bottles at the Murgo winery at Santa Venerina.*

⌒ *Up-ended bottles of sparkling wine awaiting disgorgement at the Murgo winery. Fizz and volcanic fireworks seem well suited to each other.*

⊃ Entrance to the Tenuta Scilio winery at Valle Galfina near Linguaglossa, a fine example of sensitive architectural restoration.

surrounding a lake that acts as a bird sanctuary. Overlooking it all is the huge old *palmento*, or winery, that used the gravity intrinsic to the sloping terrain to perform what today's sophisticated pumps are programmed to do.

When Cesarò turned his attention to the abandoned vineyard in 1990 he made some remarkable discoveries, fully befitting the mysterious nature of Mount Etna. Most significantly, from mid-November to late March every year the vineyard became submerged with water, without apparently causing damage to the vines. Moreover, the vines appeared to be almost two hundred years old, which meant they had survived the phylloxera outbreak of the early 20th century. The pest that causes this disease cannot, in fact, survive in sand or water. This in its turn implied that the Gurrida vinestock was uniquely original, since post philloxera viticulture has relied on pest-resistant American vinestock onto which the different grape varieties have been grafted. As the vineyard was cleaned and pruned, Cesarò saw that the original alberello training system, based on a sturdy, short, self-

⊃ Vineyards on the beautifully positioned Scilio estate where the views sweep across the valley to the Nebrodi mountains.

supporting trunk that could carry the weight of the seasonal growth, had been adapted in the 1950s to a trellised system. Moreover, the Grenache that had been planted there had over the decades been reproduced by propagation, so that here and there the secular mother plants were still visible.

As soon as the vineyard was once more in condition to produce small amounts of good fruit, Cesarò started experimenting with vinification under the guidance of Giancarlo Giurletti, an oenologist from the mountainous Trentino region in northern Italy. It was soon established that the risk of tardy frosts in spring, a common occurrence at this altitude, could be partly contained by leaving an extra late bud on the vine to germinate if the first buds froze in the tail end of winter.

The wine now produced at the Gurrida estate (40,000 bottles for the 2001 vintage) is a red with intense, composite aromas, plenty of red fruit and a long, velvety finish. Though it is not aged in wood, it has the structure and strength to marry well with mature cheeses, game

and cold cuts. To honour the man who had the Grenache vines planted in this area, Cesarò has called what is effectively a wondrous wine *Victory*, the name of Lord Nelson's ship at the battle of Trafalgar. While the grape varieties grown on Mount Etna are still predominantly the indigenous Nerello Mascalese, Nerello Cappuccio and Carricante, a little Chardonnay grown on east and north facing slopes provides Benanti with an interesting blending partner for Carricante. *Edèlmio Vino Bianco di Sicilia IGT* has just the right acidity to balance the aromas of ripe apple, citrus and almond. Murgo produces as IGTs a pleasant Chardonnay and an elegant Cabernet Sauvignon, while both Tenuta Scilio and Garruda are expecting interesting results from their recently planted Merlot. Merlot also plays a major role in the *Barone di Villagrande Sciara IGT*, in blend with Nerello Mascalese.

The point is, of course, that Chardonnay and Merlot, or indeed Grenache, grown on the side of the volcano are bound to produce wines that are highly distinctive. As the Ancients knew, the Elements speak for themselves. In this case, wine is their mouthpiece.

Messina as a Footnote, at Least for Now

Nerello Mascalese and Nerello Cappuccio, along with Nocera and a small percentage of Nero'dAvola and Gaglioppo (a variety originating in Calabria, across the straits on mainland Italy), also go into making the wines typical of Messina, the most easterly promontory of Sicily that may one day be linked to the "continent" by a bridge.

Though winemaking in this area dates back to antiquity, and in the 19th century brought considerable prosperity to the district, today it lacks a true identity and is rarely equated with quality, despite the valid efforts of wineries such as Palari, and to some extent Colosi, Grasso and Cambria as well.

Though much of the local production goes into blends made elsewhere, both in Sicily and beyond, there is actually a Messina-based appellation: the red Faro DOC, established back in 1976 and produced on the hillsides overlooking the narrow stretch of water that divides Sicily from the mainland. The province is also home to vine nurseries that supply regional growers with ready grafted varietals.

The Lesser Islands: Pantelleria and Salina

Small Worlds, Big Wines

Small though they may be, both Pantelleria and Salina are universes in their own right when it comes to their wines. Each has a specific identity that owes little, or nothing, to the nearest part of mainland Sicily. Of volcanic origin, both islands have characteristic soils that are mineral-rich, fertile and friable. The vineyards tend to be small, and practically hewn by hand over the centuries into narrow terraces tucked into the hillsides and overlooking an azure sea.

Yet despite their common vocation for producing exquisite dessert wines, and the pungent, flavoursome capers that grow abundantly on both islands, the two also differ in many respects. From the viticultural point of view, each is the haven of a different grape variety: the Zibibbo, or Muscat of Alexandria in the case of Pantelleria; and on Salina the smaller white Malvasia grape.

Moreover, Pantelleria is windswept throughout the year, to the extent that all plants, including trees, grow close to the ground or must be surrounded by walls to avoid being uprooted. While the eye gets used to seeing the sturdy, low-cropped vines with their thick horizontal branches, it comes as something of a surprise to

⮿ Muscat of Alexandria grapes (also known as Zibibbo) drying in the sun at Marco De Bartoli's Bukkuram winery on Pantelleria. The wall absorbs the heat of the sun during the day and continues to emanate warmth at night.

behold a knee-high olive tree covering an expanse of several metres, and well laden with fruit to boot. By contrast, Salina is caressed by the gentle breezes from which the Aeolian Islands, of which it is part, derive their name: in Greek mythology, Aeolus was the god of winds.

Pantelleria

With its 83 square kilometres, this is the larger of the two islands. It is also more remote, sitting alone in the Mediterranean at some distance off the southwest coast of Sicily, over towards Tunisia.

To understand the power of nature here, it is worth visiting in early spring, when the vines are still dormant. This is the season that best reveals the strength of those volcanic soils. Wild flowers grow in astounding profusion, their colours uniquely intense. Common species are as though magnified beyond all recognition, so that daisies almost appear to be dahlias.

The wineries on Pantelleria are small, and the most traditional, like those of Miceli, Marco De Bartoli and Roberto Casano of Bonsulton, are housed in *dammusi*, the slightly domed rectangular constructions that constitute the quintessential architectural genre of the island. Their origins can be traced back to the Arab occupation of the island in the 9th century. Within the thick walls of these buildings the temperature remains comfortably cool, even when sun and wind outside are searingly hot.

The finest products of the Pantelleria DOC are the Moscato and the Passito wines, both made from Zibibbo grapes. Characteristic of both are the rich aromas with a hint of apricot that, though sweet, can also surprise with a clean, almost dry finish.

One of the finest producers on the island is Marco De Bartoli, an ebullient and outspoken breakaway member of one of Marsala's oldest winegrowing families. "The difference between the Moscato and the Passito is solely dictated by climatic considerations", he explains. "When the winter is cold and the post-harvest sun is

Passito di Pantelleria

🏠	Marco De Bartoli
🍾	Passito di Pantelleria DOC – white raisin wine aged for just over a year in barriques
🍇	Zibibbo (Muscat of Alexandria) 100%
⏱	10 years
🍷	Aromas of apricots and dates; ripe apricots and honey in the mouth, with a surprisingly dry, smooth finish
🍴	Fruit tarts, light creamy desserts, dry nutty biscuits, mature hard cheeses

➲ *Volcanic dry stone walls shore up the narrow terraces of Pantelleria. To the bottom right, a* dammuso, *the traditional architecture of the island.*

accompanied by the warm sirocco wind, then the grapes will dry out properly, as required for making the Passito raisin wine. The Moscato, on the other hand, is best obtained when strong sirocco winds blow on the sprouting vines in late spring and rain repeatedly wets the grapes as they dry on the vines at the end of August".

From the four hectares of the southwest-facing vineyard at his Bukkuram winery on Pantelleria De Bartoli obtains around 160 quintals (16,000 kg) of Zibibbo grapes. During the first ten days of August, about half the yield is dried out in the sun for at least three weeks. Beyond the cellar there is a long, straight dry-stone wall a little over a metre high, entirely made of black volcanic rock. The grapes are laid out on mats that run along the ground the length of the wall, which at night releases the heat

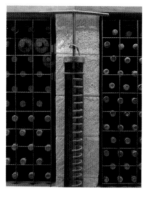

absorbed from the sun during the day, thus continuing the process of exsiccation. Every evening the grapes are turned by hand, bunch by bunch. This is a job entrusted to De Bartoli offspring, whose youthful limbs can cope with such protracted bending. It becomes a holiday task that obliging friends are roped in to help with.

The other half of the grape yield remains on the vines until September, when it is picked semi-dried, pressed and fermented. At which point the raisins produced from the sun-dried grapes are left to macerate in this wine for three months. The aim is to imbue it with the intense aromas that are typical of the island, while achieving and maintaining an ideal balance between alcohol content, sugars and fragrance. After due ageing in barriques, each year around 10,000 bottles are made, their appellation as

☊ Marco De Bartoli

☊ (Top to bottom) Early wine making equipment collected by Marco De Bartoli.

One of Pantelleria's finest products.

An ancient press displayed at Marco De Bartoli's winery museum on the Samperi estate near Marsala.

➲➲ The harvest on Pantelleria.

☊ Laying out the Zibibbo grapes to dry at Roberto Casano's Bonsulton winery on Pantelleria.

a Passito or a Moscato depending, as we have said, on the earlier vagaries of weather.

Roberto Casano of Bonsulton is also a true traditionalist, one of the last remaining commercial producers to raisin his grapes on small mounds of dried grass, which allows the warm air to reach the under side of the bunches. Locally-born Salvatore Murana is another producer whose respect for the past is legendary. The characteristic of his Martingana Passito in an aroma reminiscent of dates. By contrast, the Donnafugata winery has introduced a few small innovations when it comes to drying out the grapes. The bunches are laid out on large trays that can be placed one atop the other and turned right over, so that what was underneath faces upwards. This may not be the orthodox way of doing things, but the fact remains that the *Ben Ryè Passito* is a delightfully palatable product and a good ambassador for the island.

A couple of wineries also make interesting white table wines with the Zibibbo grapes grown on Pantelleria. One is Miceli, whose *Yrnm* is a most seductive white wine with rich fruity aromas and a long, dry finish. Another is Marco De Bartoli's *Pietra Nera*, made from grapes grown in vineyards to the north of the island, where greater shade allows for the increased acidity and lower sugars that are necessary for a fine table wine.

Salina

Compared with the isolation of Pantelleria, the north-lying island of Salina feels like a sociable sort of place, surrounded as it is by the other small islands that make up the Aeolian archipelago. At night Stromboli can be seen to the northeast, puffing its volcanic fireworks into the sky, and Lipari is clearly visible across the water on a fine day. There are numerous daily ferry connections to Milazzo, near Messina, as well as passenger ships that dock in at Lipari, the largest of the islands, before proceeding to Naples.

Although it only consists of slightly less than 27 square kilometres,

Yrnm	
🏠	Miceli
🍾	IGT – white wine aged in steel vats for at least 6 months
🍇	Zibibbo (Muscat of Alexandria) 100%
🕐	2 years
🍷	Enticingly aromatic; yet fresh, structured and persistent in the mouth
🍴	Shellfish, tasty fish such as fresh tuna, sword fish

Salina once enjoyed considerable prosperity. In the early 1800s, the fame of its capers and Malvasia raisin wine was such that it took a fleet of one hundred sailing vessels to carry the precious produce to its distant destinations. However, when the dreaded phylloxera hit the island ten years after it had laid waste to viticulture in continental Europe, it brought in its wake a radical reversal of fortunes. By the early 1900s people were leaving the island in droves. Over the next several decades the population of all the islands declined as increasing numbers left for a better life abroad, most of them in Australia.

In 1963 artist Carlo Hauner set out from his native Brescia, in northern Italy, to visit the Aeolian Islands, and was so entranced by Salina that he settled there in 1970. As he became acquainted with the local wines, he started to buy up little parcels of vineyard, and in due course was able to breathe new life into the long neglected Malvasia delle Lipari. The winery is now run by his son, who also produces table wines from grapes grown in the family vineyards and supplied by other growers.

Where once the vines on Salina were trained around a low cane pergola, they are now generally trellised for easier access to the rows. The grapes themselves are smaller than their Pantelleria counterparts, with longer, less compact bunches. The fruit to be raisined is laid out in the sun on trays, which need to be covered or brought in of an evening, once the dwindling summer days bring dew in their wake. Because of the constant dry breeze, 8 to 12 days is usually sufficient, after which temperature controlled fermentation may be protracted for as long as 3 months.

Though summer tourism has improved the financial lot of the residents of Salina, the soul of the island remains agricultural. Yet of the commercial producers of quality Malvasia, the only born and bred locals are Francesco Fenech and Antonino Caravaglio. Fenech, whose forebears actually came from Malta, passionately ekes out a living from three hectares of vineyard (another has just been planted, which is some undertaking on an island whose

⋒ The detail of this building speaks for Salina's past prosperity.

⟳ Zibibbo grapes drying in the sun on a bed of cane on Pantelleria.

⟴ Malvasia grapes ripening on Salina.

hillsides are so indented and sheer), accompanying the business of organically made Malvasia with a successful trade in salted capers. Another organic producer is the Etna-based Barone di Villagrande winery, which purchased its first parcels of vineyard on Salina several years ago and now has seven hectares in different, well-exposed locations. Their *Malvasia delle Lipari Passito* owes its being to the care and enthusiasm of Maria Nicolosi, who has produced a gloriously rich, warm golden dessert wine with aromas of broom flowers and aromatic herbs, together with hints of apricots and almonds.

In future years no doubt the Tasca d'Almerita winery will also be producing some fine examples of the Malvasia delle Lipari, having recently acquired a relatively large property lying slightly lower down than the Fenech and Villagrande vineyards. Though a certain amount of replanting will probably be necessary, so prestigious a concern with its well-established international profile is bound to help the growing revival of interest in Sicilian dessert wines.

There is talk at present, some of it heated, of creating a DOCG out of the Malvasia delle Lipari DOC. Since Salina, rather than Lipari, is the prime and original production area for this Malvasia, it would probably make sense to apply for the super category of DOCG appellation (*Denominazione d'Origine Controllata e Garantita*) for those raisin wines made with grapes grown and dried on Salina itself. This would distinguish a fine, historic product from various pale imitations, some of them grown on the neighbouring island of Lipari, which has acquired planting quotas and seems keen to sail in the wake of Salina; and some of them made on Salina itself, but with grapes purchased elsewhere in Sicily. If this is to become Sicily's first DOCG (the other contender is the Cerasuolo di Vittoria), then it is especially important to establish appropriate criteria from the outset.

⋒ *Barrels are also commonly used for ageing raisin wines.*

⮿ *The rocky descent down to the water on Salina.*

⮿ *View of the Barone di Villagrande vineyard on Salina.*

Passito

🏠 Barone di Villagrande

🍾 Malvasia delle Lipari DOC – white raisin wine

🍇 Malvasia delle Lipari 95%, Corinto Nero 5%

🕐 5–6 years

🍷 Intense aromas of broom and herbs, with a touch of ripe apricots; full and elegant in the mouth, with honeyed notes and considerable persistence

🍴 Dry nutty biscuits, simple desserts

Wine Tours of Sicily

www.vinescape.it
Get to know the wineries and landscapes of Sicily with author Kate Singleton and chef and food writer Rachel Lee. Customized tours specially designed for small groups

1. Heading Out From Palermo

Wineries

ABBAZIA DI SANTA ANASTASIA

C.da S. Anastasia
90013 Castelbuono (PA)
Tel. 0921 671959; Fax 0921672527;
www.abbaziasantanastasia.it
info@abbaziasantanastasia.it

ALESSANDRO DI CAMPOREALE

Atrio Principe di Camporeale, 8
Camporeale (PA)
Tel./Fax 0924 37238
info@alessandrodicamporeale.it

BAGLIO DI PIANETTO

Contrada Pianetto
90030 Santa Cristina Gela (PA)
Tel. 091 8570002
info@bagliodipianetto.com

AZIENDA AGRICOLA CEUSO

Baglio Ceuso
C.da Vivignato
Alcamo (TP)
Tel. 0924 22836
www.ceuso.it

CUSUMANO

C.da S. Carlo S.S. 113
Partinico (PA)
Tel. 091 8903456; Fax 091 8907933
www.cusumano.it

DUCA DI SALAPARUTA – CORVO CASA VINICOLA DI SICILIA

Via Nazionale S.S. 113
90014 Casteldaccia (PA)
Tel. 091 945111; Fax 091 953227
www.vinicorvo.it

FEOTTO DELLO JATO

C.da Feotto
San Giuseppe Jato (PA)
Tel. 091 8572650; Fax 091 8579729
www.feottodellojato.it

MICELI

Via Denti del Piraino, 7
90142 Palermo
Tel. 091 6396111; Fax 091 6396237
segreteria@midmiceli.it

POLLARA

Contrada Malvello
Monreale (PA)
Tel. 091 8462922; Fax 091 8463197
www.principedicorleone.it

RAPITALÀ

C.da Rapitalà
Camporeale (PA)
Tel. 0924 37233; Fax 0924 36115
l.guarrasi@giv.it

SPADAFORA

Contrada Virzì
Monreale (PA)
(offices) Via Ausonia, 90
90146 Palermo
Tel. 091 514952; Fax 091 6703360
www.spadafora.it

TASCA D'ALMERITA

Tenuta di Regalali
90020 Sclafani Bagni (PA)
Tel. 0921 544011; Fax 0921 542783
www.tascadalmerita.it

Tasting venues

CONVIVIUM MICELI WINE BAR

Via Generale Streva, 18
Palermo
Tel. 091 306805

Wineshop by day, winebar by night, with 300 wines of local and far-flung provenance that can be tasted by the glass, plus a further 700 by the bottle, accompanied by a fine and seasonally varied selection of cheeses, hams, etc.

ENOTECA PICONE

Via Marconi, 36
90141 Palermo
Tel. 091 331300
www.enotecapicone.it

Possibly the best selection in Sicily, fine-tuned over 3 generations of family effort.

MI MANDA PICONE

Via Alessandro Paternostro, 59
90100 Palermo
Tel. 091 6090653
www.mimandapicone.it

Begun in 2000, interesting restaurant and winebar, open evenings only.

ENOTECA VINOVERITAS

Via Sammartino, 29
Palermo
Tel. 091 6090653
info@enotecavinoveritas.it

Wine shop with an excellent selection of smaller Sicilian producers, plus a further 1500 Italian labels.

2. The West Coast: Trapani and Marsala

Wineries

ALAGNA
Via Salemi, 752
91025 Marsala (TP)
Tel. 0932 981022; Fax 0923 981302
www.alagnavini.com

ARINI
Via Salemi, 105
91025 Marsala (TP)
Tel./Fax 0923 981101
enzo@enzosalerno.it

BAGLIO HOPPS
Via Salemi – Contrada Biesina, km 12.2
91025 Marsala (TP)
Tel. 0923 967020; Fax 0923 967320
www.bagliohopps.com
info@bagliohopps.com

BAGLIO ONETO
Dei Principi di S. Lorenzo
Via delle Sirene, 8
Marsala
Tel. 0923 714328; Fax 0923 956203
www.bagliooneto.com

BAGLIO SAN VINCENZO
Via Leopardi, 11
92013 Menfi (AG)
www.bagliosanvincenzo.it

CANTINE BUFFA
Via V. Florio, 31
91025 Marsala (TP)
Tel. 0923 956748; Fax 0923 721271
www.cantinebuffa.it

CANTINE MARCO DE BARTOLI
Azienda Samperi
Contrada Fornara Samperi, 292
91025 Marsala (TP)
Tel. 0923 962093; Fax 0923 962910
www.marcodebartoli.com

DONNAFUGATA
Via Sebastiano Lipari, 18
91025 Marsala (TP)
Tel. 0923 724200; Fax 0923 722042
www.donnafugata.it

FAZIO WINES
Via Capitano Rizzo, 39
91010 Fulgatore - Erice (TP)
Tel. 0923 811700; Fax 0923 811654
www.faziowines.com

FEUDO ARANCIO
Contrada Portella Misilbesi
92017 Sambuca di Sicilia (AG)
Tel./Fax 0925 31540
www.feudoarancio.it
www.gruppomezzacorona.it

FICI
Via S. Lipari, 5
91025 Marsala (TP)
Tel. 0923 999053; Fax 0923 999511
www.cantinefici.com

FIRRIATO
Via Trapani, 4
91027 Paceco (TP)
Tel. 0923 882755; Fax 0923 883266
www.firriato.it

FLORIO
Via Vincenzo Florio, 1
91025 Marsala (TP)
Tel. 0923 781111; Fax 0923 982380
www.cantineflorio.com

FONDO ANTICO
Via Fiorame, 54/a
Fraz. Rilievo
91020 Trapani
Tel. 0923 864339; Fax 0923 865151
www.fondoantico.it

INTORCIA
Via Mazara, 10
91025 Marsala (TP)
Tel. 0923 999133; Fax 0923 999036
www.intorcia.it

MARTINEZ
Via Mazara, 209
91025 Marsala (TP)
Tel. 0923 981050; Fax 0923 721127
www.martinez.it

PELLEGRINO
Via del Fante, 37/39
91025 Marsala (TP)
Tel. 0923 719911; Fax 0923 953542
www.carlopellegrino.it

CANTINE RALLO
Via Vincenzo Florio, 2
91025 Marsala (TP)
Tel. 0923 721633; Fax 0923 721635
www.cantinerallo.it

CANTINA SOCIALE DI TRAPANI
C.da Ospedaletto
911000 Trapani
Tel. 0923 539349; Fax 0923 531007
www.cantinasocialetrapani.com

SICILIA VERA CENTONZE
Via Erice Foreste, 19
Contrada Fontanelle Ospedaletto
Via Erice Forese, 19
91100 Trapani
Tel. 0923 557513; Fax 0923 558063
siciliavera@libero.it

Tasting venues

BACCO'S
Via Trieste, 5
91025 Marsala (TP)
Tel./Fax 0923 737262
ristorantebaccos@libero.it

Slightly outside the historic centre, overlooking the coast. Intelligent cuisine and fine choice of wines. Regular tasting events featuring a menu thought up to accompany the wines of a particular producer.

IL GALLO E L'INNAMORATA

Via S. Bilardello, 18
Marsala (TP)
Tel. 329 2918503

Eight small tables, freshly made local dishes and a wine list comprising 400 Sicilian labels, plus Passito, Marsala and Malvasia. Evenings only.

FONTANA

Via S. Giovanni Bosco, 22/26
91100 Trapani
Tel. 0923 24056

Gianni Fontana's informal trattoria has an excellent wine list. Ideal place for a good lunch when you still have things to do in the afternoon.

3. The South West: Menfi, Agrigento, Licata

Wineries

CANTINA SOCIALE CELLARO

S.S. 188 – C.da Anguilla
92017 Sambuca di Siclia (AG)
Tel. 0925 941230
cellaro@futuralink.it

CANTINA SOCIALE CORBERA

Contrada Luni S.S. 188
92018 S. Margherita Belice (AG)
Tel. 0925 31377; Fax 0925 32496
corbera@tin.it

FEUDO PRINCIPI DI BUTERA

Contrada Deliella
Butera (CL)
Tel. 0934 347726; Fax 0934 347851
www.fuedobutera.it

LA LUMIA

C.da Pozzillo
92027 Licata (AG)
Tel. 0922 770057; Fax 0922 806194
www.vogliedisicilia.it

LE BOTTI DI ANTISTENE

Viale Leondardo Sciascia, 36
92100 Agrigento
Tel. 0934 939007; Fax 0934 939000
www.lebottidiantistene.com

MICELI

190 C.da Piana Scunchipani
92019 Sciacca (AG)
Tel. 0925 80188; Fax 0925 80189
See also winery head office in Itinerary 1.

G. MILAZZO

SS 123 km 12,700
92023 Campobello di Licata (AG)
Tel. 0922 878796; Fax 0922 879796
www.milazzovini.com

MORGANTE

Contrada Racalmare
92020 Grotte (AG)
Tel. 0922 945579; Fax 0922 945579
www.morgante-vini.it

PLANETA

C.da Dispensa
92013 Menfi (AG)
Tel. 091 327965; Fax 091 6124335
www.planeta.it

CANTINE SOTTESOLI (MANDRAROSSA)

SS 115
92013 Menfi (AG)
Tel. 0925 77111; Fax 0925 77142
www.cantinesettesoli.it
www.mandrarossa.it

Tasting venues

LA MADIA

C.so F. Re Capriata, 22
Licata (AG)
Tel./Fax 0922 771443;
www.ristorantelamadia.it
Tell them in advance that you want to taste a selection of the best local wines matched with a menu of their devising, and your eye, nose, palate and mind will all be gladdened.

4. The South East: Vittoria, Ragusa, Noto, Siracusa

Wineries

AVIDE

s.p.7, km 0,0
Comiso (RG)
Tel. 0932 967456; Fax 0932 731754
www.avide.it
avide@avide.it

COS

Contrada Pedalino
S.P. 4 Comiso-Caltagirone, km 8.500
97019 Vittoria (RG)
Tel. 0932 964042
Fax 0932 869700
www.cosvittoria.it

CURTO

Via Galilei 4
97014 Ispica (RG)
Tel. 0932 950161; 347 2715804
www.curto.it

GULFI

C.da Passo Guastella
97012 Chiaramonte Gulfi (RG)
Tel. 0932 921654; Fax 0932 921728
www.gulfi.it

POGGIO DI BORTOLONE

C.da Bortolone, 19
97010 Roccazzo (Fraz. Chiaramonte Gulfi) (RG)
Tel./Fax 0932 921161
www.poggiodibortolone.it

TENUTA DEL NANFRO

C.da Nanfro km 4 SP per Niscemi
95041 Caltagirone (CT)
Tel. 0933 60525; Fax 0933 60744
www.nanfro.com

PUPILLO

Contrada Targia
96100 Siracusa
Tel. 0931 494029
Fax 0931 758633
www.solacium.it

VALLE DELL'ACATE

C.da Bidini
97011 Acate (RG)
Tel. 0932 874166
Fax 0932 875114
www.valledellacate.com

Tasting venues

FATTORIA DELLE TORRI

Vico Napolitano, 14
97015 Modica (RG)
Tel./Fax 0932 751286

Impressive wine list and an inventive interpretation of local culinary custom in a delightful setting.

RISTORVIP

Via Orso Mario Corbino, 29
97100 Ragusa
Tel. 0932 652990

Enoteca.

WINE BAR ENOTECA ASSAGGIO

Via Cornelia, 32
97015 Modica (RG)
Tel. 0932 763295

Nice informal setting, with plenty of interesting things to taste, including good local wines.

BAR METRÒ

Via S. Giuliano, 44
97015 Modica (RG)
Tel. 0932 762370

Wine bar.

ENOTECA WINE BAR SAPORI DOC

C.so Umberto I, 133
Modica (RG)
Tel./Fax 0922 771443

A quiet corner for a glass of wine in a central location.

ENOTECA WINE BAR SAPORI DOC

C.so V. Veneto, 54
Pozzallo (RG)
Tel./Fax 0932 955990

5. The Volcano: Mount Etna, with a footnote on Messina

Wineries

ANTICHI VINAI

Via Castiglioni, 49
95030 Passopisciaro (CT)
Tel. 0942 983232; Fax 0942983218
www.antichivinai.it

BARONE DI VILLAGRANDE

Via del Bosco, 25
95010 Milo (CT)
Tel. 095 7082175
Fax 095 7894307
www.villagrande.it

BENANTI

Via Garibaldi, 475
95029 Viagrande (CT)
Tel. 095 7893438
Fax 095 7483436
www.vinicolabenanti.it

COTTANERA

C.da Iannuzzo
95030 Castiglione di Sicilia (CT)
Tel. 0942 963601
staff@cottanera.it

GURRIDA

S.S. 120Km 181
95036 Randazzo (CT)
Tel./Fax 095 935517
www.gurrida.it

CASA VINICOLA GRASSO

Via Albero, 5
98057 Milazzo (ME)
Tel. 090 9281082; Fax 090 9224001
casavinicolagrasso@tiscalinet.it

SCAMMACCA DEL MURGO

Via Zafferano, 13
95010 Santa Venerina (CT)
Tel. 095 950520; Fax 095 954713
www.murgo.it

TENUTA SCILIO

Viale delle Provincie, 52
95014 Giarre (CT)
Tel. 095 932822; 095 932822
scilio@infinito.it

Tasting venues

IL CARATO

Via Vittorio Emanuele II, 81
95131 Catania (CT)
Tel./Fax 095 7159247

Restaurant.

ENOTECA DEL BAGATTO

Via Regis Massimiliano, 12
98057 Milazzo (ME)
Tel. 0909 224283

CUGNO MEZZANO

Via Museo Biscari, 8
95131 Catania (CT)
Tel. 095 7158710
www.cugnomessano.it

Interesting organic restaurant with a good selection of wines, located in the historic Palazzo Biscari.

Enoteca Florio

Via Vittorio Emanuele Orlando, 129/131
95127 Catania (CT)
Tel. 095 505262
www.floriovinidafavola.it

Opened in 1993, this centrally located venue focuses on Sicilian wines, but also spreads its oenological wings further afield.

Enoteca La Nuova Cantina

Via Grasso Finocchiaro, 120
95126 Catania (CT)
Tel. 095 493860

Enoteca Regionale di Sicilia

Viale Africa, 31
95129 Catania (CT)
Tel. 095 7462210

Despite the somewhat institutional-sounding name, this is an independently run venue that selects wines from small, lesser-known Sicilian producers deserving of wider acclaim. Friday evenings are devoted to inventive interpretations of traditional cuisine accompanied by carefully selected wines. Book early: there are only 22 seats.

Enoteca Sud Est

Via A. Di Sangiuliano, 171
95131 Catania (CT)
Tel. 095 315583

Enoteca Il Tocco di VIno

Via Galatea, 18/20
95024 Acireale (CT)
Tel. 095 7634215
www.iltoccodivino.com

Sommelier Camillo Privitera's wine shop is unique for its genre in this pleasant baroque town just north of Catania.

Enoteca Voglia di Vino

Via F. Crispi, 236
Catania (CT)
Tel. 095 537178
www.enotecavogliadivino.it

Proprietors Giuseppe and Santi, both of them trained sommeliers, also host tasting events here.

Osteria I Tre Bicchieri

Via San Giuseppe al Duomo, 31
95124 Catania (CT)
Tel. 095 7153540; Fax 095 2500712
www.osteriaitrebicchieri.it

This very upmarket restaurant and wine bar belongs to Giuseppe Benanti, whose passion is wines (he owns the excellent Benanti winery on Mount Etna) and core business is pharmaceuticals. The wine list (international, Italian and Sicilian) is pretty impressive.

Ristorante Il Cuciniere
(at the Katane Palace Hotel)

Via Finocchiaro Aprile, 110
95129 Catania (CT)
Tel. 095 7470702; Fax 095 7470172

This is where Carmelo Chiaramonte, one of the most interesting younger stars in the Sicilian culinary firmament, conjures up some highly distinctive cuisine, with a good selection of Sicilian wines, especially Nero d'Avolas, to match.

6. The Lesser Islands: Pantelleria and Salina

Wineries

Abraxas

C. da Bukkuram
91017 Pantelleria (TP)
Tel./Fax 091 6110051
customer@winesabraxas.com

Bonsulton srl

Contrada Bukkuram Bonsulton 10,d
91017 Pantelleria (TP)
Tel. 338 3553041

Cantine Marco De Bartoli

Azienda Bukkuram
Contrada Bukkuram, 9
91017 Pantelleria (TP)
Tel. 0923 918344
www.marcodebartoli.com

Case di Pietra

C.da Nikà
91017 Pantelleria (TP)
Tel./Fax 06 42012644
www.casedipietra.com

Hauner

Via Umberto 1°
98050 Lingua Salina (ME)
Tel. 090 9843141; Fax 090 922665

Miceli

C.da Rekale
91017 Pantelleria (TP)
Tel. 0923 916616; Fax 0923 916153
See also winery head office in Itinerary 1.

Nuova Agricoltura

C.da Barone
91017 Pantelleria (TP)
Tel. 0923 915712; Fax 0923 691009
nuovagricoltura@pantelleria.it

Solidea

Contrada Kaddiuggia
91017 Pantelleria (TP)
Tel./Fax 0923 913016
www.solideavini.it

7. Off the beaten wine track

Maurigi

C.da Budonetto
94015 Piazza Armerina (EN)
Tel. 091 321788; 0935 85240; Fax 091 6090871
www.maurigi.it

Index